# NEW HOPE FOR DIVORCED CATHOLICS

# New Hope for Divorced Catholics

## Father Barry Brunsman

*1817*

HARPER & ROW, PUBLISHERS, SAN FRANCISCO

New York, Grand Rapids, Philadelphia, St. Louis
London, Singapore, Sydney, Tokyo

FIRST HARPER & ROW PAPERBACK EDITION PUBLISHED IN 1989.

Library of Congress Cataloging-in-Publication Data

Brunsman, Barry
    New hope for divorced Catholics.

    Bibliography: p.
    1. Divorce—Religious aspects—Catholic Church.
    2. Remarriage—Religious aspects—Catholic Church.
    3. Catholic Church—Doctrines.   I. Title.
    BX2254.B78 1985      261.8'3589        85-42770
    ISBN 0-06-061147-2
    ISBN 0-06-061146-4 (pbk.)

89  90  91  92  93 MCN  10  9  8  7  6  5  4  3  2  1

# Contents

## A NOTE TO THE READER

All names, characteristics, and background details in the cases and examples presented in this book have been changed. In addition, several cases in the book—although true to my experience—are wholly fictitious.

# Introduction

Today's Christian community faces a crisis—the epidemic of marriage failures. The divorce rate is high, but divorce is not the only result of marriage failure. Pain and anguish are also felt by those who suffer from estrangement, abandonment, separation, and mutual tolerance. Statisticians dealing with marriage and divorce place the total number of marriage tragedies, which includes disappearance, estrangement, and mutual tolerance, at eighty percent.

The Christian community must deal with a severe dilemma. How can it uphold Jesus' banner of the indissolubility of marriage and still minister to the parties of broken marriages? The danger of hypocrisy is ever present. This dilemma particularly involves the Roman Catholic Church, one of the most vocal and absolute of the Christian bodies about the indissolubility of marriage. Yet a reliable estimate of the number of Roman Catholics touched by divorce or by remarriage is over eight million, a fact cited as the greatest reason for the loss of membership in the Catholic Church today. Over fifty percent of Catholics leaving the Church attribute their exit to the conflict between their personal experience of divorce and remarriage and the Church's rigid stand on the issue.

The Catholic Church has over two thousand years of experience in its storehouse. Like a good steward, the Church might well bring out the old as well as the new and find in its own history solutions to the present agonizing predicament.

Church law and hierarchy often demand uniformity, a form of regimentation seemingly easier to deal with than bringing about unity within diversity. Yet no other Christian church is present in such a vast number of cultures as is the Catholic Church. A person would not normally criticize a Westerner for reading a book from left to right, or a Jew for reading Hebrew from right to left, or a Chinese for doing neither. Yet marriage customs and concepts in the vast variety of cultures the Church finds itself in can differ as radically as these reading habits.

A church is both an institution and the people in it. The institution is made of traditions, codes, procedures, rituals, governing systems, and buildings. The people are those who have been baptized in this tradition and either live within it and interpret and enforce its codes or live against it, outside of it. Principally because of the people who give life to a structure, there will never be complete harmony within it; often acute tension exists between the institution and its prophets. There will be downright disagreement between those who hold "when in doubt, favor the law" and those who hold "when in doubt, favor the person."

Some people think that the Church should be made up of saints, the perfect: no hypocrisy; practice what you preach or get out. Others see the Church as an institution for and of the broken— who are hypocrites to be sure—but one that is trying to reduce their number. Some see the Church as the bride of Christ. How do you reform that? Others see the Church as a pilgrim people constantly in need of reform. Some see the Gospels and even Church laws as rules to be enforced. Others see them as ideals for inspiration, knowing that from those who have been given little, little is required. By personality, some require and are most comfortable with uniformity of practice. These people state, "No matter where we go throughout the world, the Church should always be the same." Others insist that unity, not uniformity, is the only thing the Church has ever wanted or had in its diverse cultures. The interesting fact about Catholicism is that even with this variety of cultures and lifestyles there are those members who are certain what practices are "Christian" (meaning Catholic) and what practices are not.

Theoretically, most members accept the fact that the Church is both divine and human. But, in fact, when the words "the Church says" are used, it is almost as though God is using a megaphone to talk to the people. The closer one gets to the people who make up the Church when the phrase "the Church says" occurs, the more one wonders where the divine is hiding.

This book addresses itself, then, to the challenge of proclaiming the gospel call for marriage indissolubility while, at the same time, proclaiming the worth of the divorced or remarried person. It shows the disparity between what is theologically possible for re-marriage and what the general pastoral practice is. The first topic to be addressed is the folklore or misconceptions so damaging to the full practice of the Catholic faith of those who are remarried or even just divorced. So much time in ministry must be spent just demythologizing religious clichés that are passed down from fa-ther to son and mother to daughter. The book then explores the root statements in Scripture regarding divorce and remarriage. The Christian practice of divorce and remarriage from the time of Jesus to the present day is then investigated. Having acquired this perspective, the book then synopsizes and analyzes four major historical viewpoints on the issue of remarriage. The concluding chapter lists many of the growing ministries to the divorced in the Catholic Church of the United States.

*New Hope for Divorced Catholics* is the result of a doctoral disserta-tion written in 1984. Many statements are from interviews with noted canon lawyers and moral theologians. The purpose of the book is to establish the fact that separation from full communion with God and Church practice for the divorced and remarried only occurs in the misapplication of religious concepts or an adherance to severity for the sake of example.

Clearly stated:

- A divorced Catholic can never be prohibited from receiving Communion.

- A sincere Catholic remarried "outside the Church" can never be prohibited from receiving Communion. With competent clerical or lay help, or even this book, a person could make a decision concerning the termination of a previous marriage either by the sin theory, the death theory, the annulment theory, or the preference principle theory and enter a lawful second marriage. Even if this determination is absent, accord-ing to the explicit declaration of the Sacred Congregation in Rome (March 21, 1975), a remarried Catholic could be admit-ted to the sacraments.

- A second marriage can be sacred in the Roman Catholic Church without an annulment of the first.

# Invocation
# "Let My People Go!"

Probably the greatest agony for a priest who is aware of the full canonical and pastoral redemption and care of the Church for broken people is to encounter those who have been victims of the inadequate or even incorrect presentation of the ecclesiastical process. Sometimes these people are victims because of the decade of history in which they were born. The Church, like any parent, at times looks back on the direction and care of its children with grave misgivings. But that is hindsight! At the time, it was doing the very best it knew; but it was wrong. Changes occur, and parents are often not the first to see them. A child innocently remarks, "It's not that way anymore, Mom. Everybody . . ." However, Mom did not see the change. As the saying goes, everyone deserves better parents. But that's the human condition. Some even say parents deserve better children. But that's also the human condition. Part of Christian maturity is seeing that same human condition in the Church.

In the thirties and early forties society would not elect a divorcé as a town council member, as mayor of a city, as governor of a state, or as president of the United States. The churches, both Catholic and Protestant, were equally horrified at divorce. In the Catholic Church, annulment was virtually unheard of. The great solution of the time was the Pauline Privilege, which had its origin in the New Testament. In 1 Corinthians 7:15, St. Paul states that if a pagan divorces a Christian spouse, the baptized person is free to remarry a Christian because a contract in the Lord is higher than a human contract. When this kind of marriage failed, there was "an out." It was the luck of the draw.

Excitement in the canonical world erupted with the Helena, Montana case of this century. The excitement reached a crescendo when this was later followed by the Fresno case. This was the origin of the Petrine Privilege, also called the Privilege of the Faith.

The first exception to indissolubility of marriage was St. Paul's permission. The second was that contained in St. Matthew's gospel. The third offical exception to indissolubility is the Petrine Privilege which extended the Pauline Privilege to include a marriage in which one party was a baptized Protestant and the other was not baptized. The theory behind the privileges was that a divine relationship (baptism) would supercede a human relationship (marriage). The third privilege was called Petrine because it is not contained in scripture but is given only by virtue of the power of the successor of St. Peter to bind and to loose. This was the "needle in the haystack" solution. The priest who could facilitate a Petrine Privilege was really "the outstanding canonist." But these kinds of solutions didn't help the overwhelming majority of marriage failures, and the Church as parent also had to grow up to handle problems and challenges in new ways.

But perhaps for the priest who is knowledgeable, the most heart-rending of all are the people who are the victims of poor, if not grossly inadequate, clerical practice. It does happen, unfortunately, more than most devout Catholics would ever suspect.

The very day I am writing this, in fact just four hours ago, I went to a mobile home park to bless the marriage of Curly and Carol, a couple who have been married fifty-four years. Carol was born of French Canadian parents, of a family of very staunch and devout Catholics. In the transitional years of the thirties and forties her first marriage disentegrated, to the horror and the sworn secrecy of all the family. She had even been married in church! Curly, to whom she is now married, is a very delightful, joyful, sensitive, understanding man born of anti-Catholic parents. He never understood why his parents always talked about "those awful Catholics." Curly's first marriage did not work out. He, like his parents, divorced. Soon after the divorce, his wife disappeared. Then, in time, he met Carol. He fell deeply in love with "a Catholic" and would do anything for her.

Both of them went to a priest. The priest told them in a very courteous way that there was no hope of their marrying in the Church. Then they heard of a wonderful missionary in a neighboring parish who gave fascinating talks. To their utter shock the priest told them to get out. "You are living in sin!" he scolded.

Carol felt her first marriage was a sacrilege, not a sacrament; it was violent and disgraceful. Curly reflected on his marriage, saying that his former wife hadn't been mature enough to marry. She had slept around promiscuously; many people had called her a slut. He had had no choice but to divorce her.

"I saw no wrong in that. In fact, I thought it was the honorable thing to do. I also thought marrying Carol brought me closer to God. We really love each other. We thought God blessed us even though the Church did not understand.

"My in-laws were absolutely the most incredible, beautiful people that I have ever known. They could not come to our wedding because a priest would not perform it, but they loved us, and we loved them, anyway.

"We had three children of this marriage. We saw that they were baptized, educated in Catholic schools, and received all their sacraments. I so wanted to become a Catholic, but the Church said I was living in sin. Carol would sit in the back of the church during Mass. She was ashamed because she could not go to Communion. She never missed a Mass. I would take her and want to stay with her, but I could not endure her agony. So I used to walk outside the church, asking God to send help. I made long trips over to the Fresno chancery office pleading for some help.

"My mother, who was nonreligious, was angry when the priest interviewed her for our marriage case. For some reason, she told the priest that I was christened, that is, baptized. To be fair about this whole thing, one of the priests rode way back into the mountains just to interview my mother. It must have taken him all day. My mother lied for some reason. I have never been baptized.

"Carol's former husband had died by this time, so she was free to remarry. However, because my mother testified that I was christened, I was told by the bishop's office that there was no hope. Besides that, they could not even find my former wife because she drifted so much. Probably the hardest days of my life were the First Communion events of our children, and both of us were not able to go to Communion. Though I loved the Catholic Church, I could not join because I was a sinner.

"When the diocese was moved to Monterey from Fresno, I thought I might have another chance. I drove over there and presented the priest my problem. He seemed rather optimistic about my case, but when he got our file, this thing that my mother brought up about christening came back to haunt us. She never went to church in her life. The priest told me that there was no hope.

"On one of the other occasions when I took Carol to Mass, I remember hearing the priest say something about people having to carry their cross in life in order to be more like Jesus. Oddly enough, I felt the Church rules were unfair and were my cross, but I would carry it for Jesus. When the kids were married and Carol was not able to go to Communion, that was my cross. When Carol's parents died, and everyone went to Communion and we could not, that was my cross. On Christmas and Easter I would go to Mass with Carol, and when I would look over and her eyes were filled with tears at Communion time, that was my cross. I guess when I thought the cross would break me was when one of our children died. Again, Carol could not go to Communion. Neither could I. But our kids could.

"At the receptions and the parties after these events, I think I was a good host. People would say I was so affable, jovial, and loving. I wanted to cry, because I would look across the room and Carol was so gracious, pleasant, and caring. I knew those were appearances that hid a broken heart.

"I'm so happy, Father, that you can bless our marriage now. I know that it will be wonderful for Carol. I only wish her parents were able to be here. They prayed for this day until the very day they died. I hope they know about it now. We're going to call our kids tonight. One has been a little bitter toward the Church, so we do not know how he will take this news. We know the other one will be extremely happy.

"I know Carol is afraid of confession. She said she doesn't know how to go anymore. She hasn't been in fifty-four years. As for me, I would like to be baptized, but I know I can't. I'm too old to learn the catechism. I hope I can be buried with her."

I blessed their marriage in the front room of the mobile home. Afterward I ate their simple cake and toasted them with champagne. I smiled and laughed with them.

I came back to the rectory, and the secretary called out that there were some maintenance problems that were rather urgent. All I could say was, "Give me twenty minutes." I went to my back bedroom, put the prayer book and stole on my desk, dropped onto the bed, and cried. I had one prayer to God—the prayer of Moses when he saw his people in bondage: "Let my people go!"

The tragic aspect of this story is that it is not an isolated instance; the number of similar cases is countless.

# 1. Folklore: Popular and Widespread Misconceptions About Divorce and Remarriage

Folklore is the traditional customs and tales or superstitions preserved orally among the people. Folklore is fascinating because it often portrays or betrays the spirit of the people. In the last century the folklore surrounding divorce and remarriage in the Christian tradition has usually been derived from a puritanical source. It is closer to superstition than the teaching of the Church. Its religious spirit is severely pessimistic and it contains stories about all those people who lost their heavenly destiny in the last moments of life.

If, however, the religious atmosphere is merciful, then neither life nor death nor anything can separate us from the love of God. Religious models of both severity and mercy existed in the early Church and still remain in the Church today. Since the overwhelming number of religious customs are not scriptural but cultural, the model and spirit of the assembly will determine whether a severe or merciful judgment is rendered. If the Church is for the perfect, then human error is generally handled severely. If the Church is for the sick and the poor, then human error is generally handled with love and mercy.

In the United States the early religions were fairly severe. According to Puritan, Calvinistic, Irish or Prussian religious thought, divorce was a horror. Remarriage was the abomination of abominations. In some religious groups there was forgiveness for neither. This may have reflected the spirit of Church people, but in most cases it did not reflect the official teaching.

In 1978, a group of conscientious, divorced Catholics in Las

Vegas wanted to initiate a support group for themselves. A priest who had worked a great deal with the divorced was asked to present three talks on the Church's position and care of the divorced.

The priest began in a rather unique manner. He thanked the leaders for inviting him to speak on the Church's position about the divorced and praised them for their efforts to establish a much-needed support group in the area. He then said that people often go to lectures not realizing the ideas they have already formulated in their minds on the topic. He stated that overlays on already formulated ideas or emotional experiences are automatically rejected because they do not match what is already there. So he asked his audience of over one hundred to close their eyes and relax. He directed them to be still within themselves. The priest then announced that he was going to give them a word and asked them to interiorize it and identify the feeling it evoked. There were a few seconds of quiet. The priest then said the word "Church." There was a stillness in the room. "A feeling is just one word," he said. "What are you feeling?" A lover of the Church would have been in utter shock. Like popcorn popping, soft responses came one after another from the audience: "rejection," "hurt," "cruel," "not understanding," "bitter," "demanding," "legalistic," "confused," "sorrow," "ignorant." No one vocalized a positive emotion. The priest then asked them to sit up and open their eyes.

Humorously he said, "I've just decided something. I'm going home." He then went on to say that through education he might be able to alter their minds about the Church in its pastoral care of the divorced. However, he was doubtful about changing their hearts because the Church was really people like themselves, who, out of fear, hurt, or failure, perpetuated all of those feelings.

The negative feelings about the Church harbored by this group of divorced Catholics in many cases reflect the damage done by inaccurate beliefs and practices. Priests, ministers, and counselors often become exhausted in listening to and demythologizing the same hurt-filled statements of the divorced. These comments are not restricted to older Catholics but are equally present among the younger set. Let's take a look at some of the misconceptions.

## EXCOMMUNICATION

"A divorced person is excommunicated." False. "A divorced and remarried Catholic is excommunicated." Also false.

The most damaging of all misconceptions about divorce and remarriage is the one about excommunication. Why Roman Catholic clergy and laity were ever so cruel as to further degrade an already broken person is beyond understanding. The Council of Baltimore in 1843 did place excommunication upon divorce, but forty-one years later, seeing that this was far too severe, the Third Plenary Council of Baltimore of 1884 withdrew the censure. This plenary council stated that if a person married "outside the Church *out of defiance,*" such a person would be excommunicated. It would take a real stretch of the imagination to see a person entering marriage with such an intention. What was cruel was the interpretation that excommunication was extended to every Roman Catholic whose second marriage was "outside the Church." Perhaps the saddest thing in this whole issue is that the thousands of remarried Catholics who were so labeled by the Church tribunals and clergy were refused a justified annulment process by the very same people.

This humanmade censure of excommunication conveyed more damnation for the divorced Catholic than ever appears in the very words of Jesus. Because of it, thousands upon thousands of Catholics in second marriages agonized, felt excommunicated, and did not go to Communion or church for the rest of their lives when, in fact, they were in the good graces of the Church. This love and kindness towards a divorced person is also explicitly expressed in Pope John Paul II's "Apostolic Exhortation on the family" (15 December 1981): "Together with the synod, I earnestly call upon pastors and the whole community of the faithful to help the divorced and with solicitous care to make sure that they do not consider themselves as separated from the church, for a baptized persons they can and indeed must share in her life. They should be encouraged to listen to the Word of God, to attend the sacrifice of the Mass, to persevere in prayer, to contribute to works of charity, and to community efforts in favor of justice, to bring up their children in the Christian faith, to cultivate the spirit and practice of penance and thus implore, day by day, God's grace. Let the Church pray for them, encourage them, and show herself a merciful mother and thus sustain them in faith and hope."

The Catholic community will never be able to repair the untold damage this has cost. To put a stop to the spread of this damaging misconception, which occurred especially in the United States, in 1977 the American bishops rescinded the directive of the Council of Baltimore of 1884. This was further affirmed by Rome the following year.[1]

## CHURCH WEDDINGS ARE VALID

"All Church marriages are valid before God." False.

The Church's annulment process officially proclaims that not every marriage "in the Church" is valid. On a scholarly level, since a sacramental marriage involves a covenant with God and the proclamation of that before the community, the real question is how many Church marriages really are valid. One priest-psychologist shocked a clergy audience by saying that he believed that eighty percent of the marriages in the Catholic Church today were not valid. The reason he gave was that most couples know that divorce is an option; they live in a culture of temporary vocations and are incapable of a once-only commitment.

## CONFUSION ABOUT VALIDITY

"Any Catholic marriage can be considered for annulment." False.

The annulment process looks at the marriage only at the very time of the wedding. If a marriage had all the elements of validity at the time of its performance, an annulment is not possible. Other solutions must be used in those cases. Often a marriage might be valid or invalid before God, but humans have no way of knowing which it is. When there is total confusion about the validity of a marriage, Church law allows the person to make a choice and get on with life.

In January of 1983 in Boston, a member of a tribunal who also doubled as the pastor of a parish church was visited by a middle-aged couple who wanted to be married. In interviewing them, he asked if either of them had been married before. The answer was yes. The priest graciously asked if they would share the background history of their marriages. With hesitation, both agreed.

The man mentioned that he had a previous marriage and that his wife had been tragically killed in an automobile accident. He went on to say that the marriage was almost at an end before her death, since he was an alcoholic. Since then he had joined AA, and that is where he met Linda, whom he now wanted to marry. The priest thanked him for sharing and then turned to Linda.

"And have you been married before, Linda?" the priest asked.

Hesitantly she said, "Yes, I have." Perhaps her hesitancy prompted the question, "Was it more than once?"

She smiled and said, "Yes, Father, ten times."

The priest blinked and his jaw dropped visibly. He asked, "Are you joking?"

She said, "No, Father, I am not joking. I was an alcoholic from the time I was eighteen years old. I only know six of the husbands I married. I was completely drunk for four of them. They were only of short terms. I do not have any idea where those people are or even what their names are."

With a delightful sense of humor the priest laughed and gently said, "You've had an interesting marital career."

All three laughed and she went on to say, "I have been sober for four years, and Richard and I have been going with each other for two years. As startling as my marriage career has been, I honestly feel I've never been married. I think this is the first time I have ever been sober enough to really love someone. I am fascinated by my feelings for Richard, and at forty-seven years old I find myself in love for the first time. Is there a possibility that we can get married in church?"

The priest looked like an archeologist who had just found a rare artifact. He smiled and said, "Absolutely. You will be able to, but first of all I have a friend who is a judge and director of the tribunal. He loves detail and I am deliriously curious as to what he would say to this case. Would you mind if I phone him?" The couple pleasantly agreed. The priest leaned back and punched the tribunal number. The couple heard the one-sided conversation.

"Hey, John, I have a case for you! There's a very delightful couple who are both a part of AA, and she has been married ten times before. She doesn't even know who four of them are. What's our flight plan with regard to all of this?" There was a listening pause. "Get all the marriage and divorce certificates! John, she doesn't even know four of the husbands." Another listening pause. "What do you mean? We'd have to put Scotland Yard on this thing." Another pause, and the priest said, "Okay, John, I'll take care of it." And he hung up.

The priest laughed and said, "He just loves detail. And challenged by the impossible, he forgot the canon law that allows a person to make a choice when it is impossible to determine who the true spouse was. Some people just love the intricacies of the law. It's like a brain game."

Turning again to the couple he asked, "When would you like to get married?"

## WEDDINGS OUTSIDE THE CHURCH

"All marriages 'outside' the Church are invalid." False.

Canon 1116 states clearly that if a Roman Catholic cannot get access to the proper authority for a marriage within thirty days, he or she may use any authority. If a person has a legitimate right to marry by Church law but is refused, he or she can have the wedding anywhere and remain within the Church.

A priest whose brother was seeking an annulment in a diocese in the West questioned the long delay. He contacted the tribunal and was told that when a marriage was submitted for an annulment, it was given a year's waiting time to assure the fact that the divorce was really final. The priest had worked with several dioceses in the annulment process and he responded, "Are you aware that such an arbitrary delay violates canon law and gives to every requesting person permission to marry anywhere?" Having been made aware of this, the diocese changed its policy.

In the early sixties in the predominantly Italian parish of St. George's in Seattle, Washington, the young associate pastor ran into some embarrassing situations. Several decades before his time, Italians from the old country had migrated into the lower Seattle area. The lowlands of that area were ideal for truck farming. In those early times, there were no Italian priests to follow this unusually large immigration. Not being able to speak the language, people simply went to the justice of the peace to be married. Even in many of these civil marriages, the records were very poorly entered and often incomplete because of the language barrier.

Forty years later, an Italian priest was brought in to give a parish mission for the Italians of that area. Beside ranting and raving about sin and damnation, he condemned those who had never been married "in the Church." When the Italian priest was spotted coming down the street for home visits, in their typical peasant, earthy style, these folk were never home. However, the young associate fared better with them. Though his discussion of theology was limited by the Italian custom of drinking wine with an honored guest, he tried to convince them that their marriages were valid. The Church allowed civil marriages when there was no access to a priest. However, they believed that they had to be married by a priest before they could go to Communion again. So the young associate arranged a time when he "blessed" their marriages so they could feel better.

Sons and daughters, grandchildren and friends all gathered together for the gala celebration of grandma and grandpa "getting married." It was a great celebration for all present, with food in endless variety and wine in limitless abundance. It was a gala celebration for everyone except the young priest who, in a very loving way, proclaimed that the marriage was truly a marriage many years ago. Grandma and grandpa were going to renew their vows in thanksgiving for their many years of marriage. The priest was red with embarrassment lest they think their children were not legitimate, but these folk never doubted that. They were so happy to gather for a family celebration. Oh and, yes, they could go to Communion again.

## LEGITIMACY OF CHILDREN

"An annulment makes the children bastards." False.

There are no illegitimate children before God. Every person is made in the image and likeness of God. Illegitimacy has to do with civil rules. If the couple had a civil license, the children are forever legitimate. It would be irresponsible to consider children illegitimate for religious reasons when the concept is a civil one.

## CHURCH BURIAL

"A person in an invalid marriage cannot be buried from the Church." False.

Burial from the Church is not a pronouncement of a person's destiny. God alone can make that decision. One of the Christian virtues is to bury the dead.

## COMMUNION

"A person in an invalid marriage cannot go to Communion." False.

If the Church exists to minister to the sick and the poor, then those invalidly married certainly could go to Communion. If in the Church Communion is a reward for the perfect, only then is it hard to proclaim who can go to Communion.[2]

The official law of the Church in Canons 912 and 915 indicates that it is possible for people in invalid remarriages to receive Communion. The first says that any baptized person can receive Communion. The second canon maintains that Communion can only be refused to someone who has been excommunicated or who is under interdict after the penalty has been inflicted or who obstinately persevers in grave sin. The mind of the law is that all prohibitive or penal canons have to be interpreted in the narrowest sense.[3] This is indicated in Rome's 1973 and 1975 responses concerning the internal forum (Sacrament of Reconciliation). The 1975 response is:

. . . These couples may be allowed to receive the sacraments on two conditions, that they try to live according to the demands of Christian moral principles and that they receive the sacraments in churches where in which they are not known so that they will not create any scandal.[4]

The popular belief that a person who is in an invalid marriage cannot go to Communion reflects more the spirit of one who punishes or wants to be punished rather than the mind of the Church.

## BAPTISMAL SPONSOR

"The divorced person cannot be a sponsor for baptism." False. Today a Protestant can be selected as a Christian witness for a Catholic baptism. Many moralist theologians see in this permission *a fortiori* for a remarried Christian Catholic to stand in for baptism. It is of interest that the Protestant Christian witness is almost never asked about his or her Sunday practice or former marriages, while the Catholic is often made to give an account of his or her stewardship and even asked to obtain written permission from the home parish prior to being accepted as a baptismal sponsor.

## MARRIAGE WITNESS

"A divorced person cannot witness a Catholic marriage." False. Witnessing a marriage is not a religious statement. Witnessing a marriage is simply the affirmation that the persons have a right to get married according to state laws.

## REMARRIAGE AND LAY MINISTRY

"A divorced person cannot assume leadership in the Church, that is, as a member of a parish council, lector, teacher of religion, and so forth." It depends. There is no Church law on such issues. The question is decided according to the leadership or spirit of a particular community. Is the Church for the perfect or the broken?

## BAPTISM OF CHILDREN

"Catholics in invalid marriages cannot have their children baptized." False. The concept of baptism today is that a child is baptized when the family, principally the parents, can provide models for religion and faith. Deep faith is a very powerful teacher whether it is shown by the "perfect" Catholic or someone in an invalid marriage. The faith witness of those who thought they were excommunicated and yet continued going to Mass on Sunday or even daily was profound.

## ANNULMENTS AND MONEY

"You can get an annulment only if you have money." False.

The lack of money should not be an obstacle for securing an annulment. The priest has only to indicate the applicant's inadequate financial means and the annulment will be processed without charge. This misconception often indicates either serious ignorance or anger toward the Church for some other reason. The Church annulment process is usually more humane and less expensive than any civil divorce. Yet, by the same token, members of the Church have a moral responsibility to support stenographers, notaries, and other people involved in the process.

## ANNULMENTS WITH CHILDREN

"A marriage with children cannot be annulled." False.

The Church's annulment process has to do with the marital capability of the man and woman at the time of the wedding. Children have nothing to do with the validity or invalidity of a marriage.

## ANNULMENTS AND FAVORITISM

"If you know someone important, you can get an annulment." False.

The spirit behind this belief is an accusation that those involved in the process are arbitrary and have no accounting before God. It is too bad God does not come down to judge every case personally. We have to depend on humans to do it. Any Church official, however, has someday to account to the God who said, "What I have put together, let no one put asunder." But Catholics seeking an annulment definitely would have more success if they sought out a priest who is both familiar with the process and has the time to expedite it. The local parish priest may be a very holy man and a supreme liturgist, but he may have no expertise with canon law.

And some priests don't like the annulment process and consequently tend to procrastinate in it.

## ANNULMENTS TAKE YEARS

"Annulments take many years to process." Generally speaking, false.
The annulment cases that are accepted usually have equal or better processing time than most civil divorces. In both cases a great deal depends upon cooperation of the spouses and the case loads of those doing the processing.

## PROTESTANT MARRIAGE AND VALIDITY

"A Protestant marriage is not valid because it is outside the Catholic Church." False.
This idea has been highly damaging to the ecumenical spirit, because it indicates an unparalleled arrogance on the part of Catholics to pass judgment on marriages in other religions. The truth is that Protestant couples are urged to go to their own church for their wedding. Such an idea has thundering ramifications when a Catholic party brings his or her formerly married Protestant friend for a marriage arrangement in the Catholic Church. It is usually prefaced with the words, "Father, my friend is a Protestant. He [or she] has been married before but not in the Catholic Church." But the Protestant's former marriage is presumed valid unless proven otherwise.

## SPOUSE MUST COOPERATE IN AN ANNULMENT

"An annulment requires the cooperation of the spouse." False. Most tribunals will process an annulment on the statement of a single partner, plus witnesses, if the spouse refuses to participate in the process.

## CONCLUSIONS

Probably one of the most painful experiences for a person involved in the ministry to the divorced and remarried is to witness the damage caused by misconceptions about the Church's position. Not only is so much psychic energy spent on educating and demythologizing, it is particularly heartbreaking to see the devout suffer. For example, to see someone go to Mass faithfully for thirty, forty, or fifty years without receiving Communion because of misinformation. Then the ministering person knows the meaning of the phrase "the truth will set people free."

# 2. Scripture: What the Bible Really Teaches About Marriage

The words of Jesus in the New Testament are our guide to under-. standing divorce and remarriage in the Christian tradition. During the journey into the richness of these Scripture passages, it is imperative to keep two things in mind: first, how is Scripture being read? Second, what is the manner in which it is to be applied? Without the awareness of these two issues, there will be nothing but chaos and disharmony in an already painful part of Christian life. Why? Because there is some legitimate leeway in interpreting the five main New Testament passages on marriage and divorce. The finest biblical scholars, both Catholic and Protestant, have never reached a consensus on the exact meaning of the passages. The Catholic Church has never officially defined their sense.[1]

## HOW THE SCRIPTURES CAN BE READ

A fundamentalist approach is taken by many Christians who believe that Scripture should be lived literally. These literalists look upon Scripture as the exact word of God. Their viewpoint is that the words of Jesus are literal, verbatim recordings of what he said and are binding as is.

Parallelists insist that if you take one passage of Scripture, you must also include all those that are similar to it in subject matter. They, like the literalists, believe that Scripture is the word of God, but it is only looking at the collage of parallel passages that leads to an understanding of God's revelation. Their way of arriving at the truth of Scripture is more holistic than that of most literalists. Scripture to this group is normative.

Scholars adhering to a form-critical approach maintain that the writers of Scripture were authors addressing real-life situations. These scholars maintain that the true meaning of the words of revelation can only be ascertained by studying the culture of Jesus and the people to whom the words were addressed. Some even see the early Christian community influencing the writing of Scripture. These scholars or readers are repelled by the literalist's approach, amused by the parallelist's and only satisfied by knowing the real-life situation in which the words were spoken and later recorded.

Traditionalists are sensitive to the way the Christians have lived out the words of Scripture over the centuries in prayers, feast days, customs, and other devotions. They, like the others, see Scripture as the word of God. Meaningful to them are the words "many are the things that you cannot understand now, but when the Spirit comes . . . "

Each of these viewpoints has an interesting dimension. Each uses the same Scripture, yet each may come out with decisively different conclusions about the way Scripture is applied.

## HOW THE SCRIPTURES CAN BE APPLIED

The findings of these different viewpoints can be applied in one of two ways: Scripture is seen either as a moral imperative (absolute) or as an ideal.

Individuals who see Scripture as a moral imperative are principally found among the literalists. The word of God is absolute; it is to be applied absolutely for all people at all times in all cultures. Other individuals see Scripture as an ideal and insist that Jesus' call to holiness was an invitation and not a demand. They insist that Jesus ate and drank with sinners and even maintained that prostitutes and streetwalkers would enter the kingdom of heaven.

In the issue of divorce and remarriage, there is no question in the minds of either group that Jesus' teaching on marriage was that it is indissoluble. Both understand that all marriages are called to be permanent relationships. The first group, however, insists that all those who marry must abide by the rules under pain of sin. The second group insists that the permanent relationship is the ideal. "When much has been given a man, much will be required of him. More will be asked of a man to whom more has been entrusted" (Luke 12:48). Generally speaking, the literalists, more certain of

what God intends through Scripture, insist on the moral imperative position; while those of the form-critical school, forced to see
different trends and viewpoints in scripture, view scripture as having an element of the ideal.

By personality, people have a tendency to gravitate toward
one or the other group. This certainly influences any conclusions
they draw. Scholars write from one or the other context. Most
Scripture scholars, both Catholic and Protestant, write out of the
framework of either form criticism or the traditionalist approach.
Virtually all of these employ the method of the parallelists as
a matter of course. Supporters of the literalist approach who
are classified as scholars concentrate more on the actual word
derivation.

The position of Catholic priests in the ministry is a very perplexing one in the issue of divorce and remarriage. In the realm
of theological speculation and even among the canon law scholars, Scripture is generally taken as an ideal to be administered
with mercy and understanding. In practice, however, on the diocesan and parochial levels, there is a firm tendency to take Scripture as a moral imperative exacting from the divorced stringent
obedience to Church norms. In many cases, especially for those
remarried without the Church's blessing, there is no forgiveness.
Priests do know the full liberty of the Church's law, but they are
afraid to be open about encouraging formerly married Catholics
to follow what they believe is true before God. In the priest's
training, this flexibility is called the "pastoral solution." Although it recognizes that Jesus strongly advocated permanency
of marriage, it also acknowledges that the divorced and remarried have as much right to the sacraments as others. Such a solution is not processed by the diocesan tribunal. If a priest is "reported" for encouraging the people to use a pastoral solution, he
may be called in by the tribunal to give an account of his stewardship. Many priests even fear being suspended from priestly
activity. Yet the law of the Church and the Vaticam document
*Declaration on Religious Freedom* teach that the true conscience of a
person in a pastoral decision is a form of the Church's tribunal
*as much as* the diocesean tribunal.

## OLD TESTAMENT

In an exhaustive doctoral dissertation on covenants of the Old Testament, Dale Alfred Patrick gives a complete list of covenants.[5] Noticeably absent from the list is any mention of a covenant of marriage between two people. Polygamy appears throughout the Old Testament. In Genesis 16, Abraham, the father of the Israelites, though not married to Hagar has intercourse with her. Abraham enters this relationship at the request of his own wife, Sarah. Scripture records with censure that Jacob had two wives, Leah and Rachel. Also the great leader of Israel, King Solomon, had many wives. Deuteronomy 24 even gives instructions on how to divorce a wife. Another principal reference of allowing divorce and remarriage is Moses himself. He did allow remarriage after certain conditions were fulfilled.

However, the prophet Hosea, who wrote around 700 B.C., compares the relationship of God to his people with the bond of a married couple. As God is faithful to a straying Israel, so a married partner should be faithful to an erring spouse. Hosea's words place married love in a new light of loving fidelity. In the patriarchal society of the Jews, this remained an ideal, but it certainly was not taken as absolute.

Yahweh's relationship with the people is also compared to the relationship of husband and wife in Ezekiel 16. The relationship between Yahweh and Israel is compared to the marriage of a man who gave his wife everything, yet she deserted him.

The story of Elkanah and Hannah in the book of Samuel has similar overtones of exalting the faithful love between husband and wife. The book of Proverbs tells how wonderful it is to have only one wife. Malachi declares that divorce is evil. Tobit comes closest to the Christian view when he says that the ideal family is one wife, one husband. None of these examples, however, indicates a covenant relationship, nor do they prohibit divorce.

## NEW TESTAMENT

In the award-winning book *Divorce and Remarriage in the Catholic Church,* Lawrence Wrenn, its editor, brought together in 1974, the writings of outstanding scholars on this subject. George MacRae, S.J., a Scripture scholar, was asked to respond to the massive amount of exegesis on the five main New Testament passages concerning divorce and remarriage. He writes:

. . . we will try to avoid becoming mired in exegetical detail and conjectures; in this question, more than any others, exegetical ingenuity has obscured what is really present in the New Testament itself.[6]

The passages on divorce and remarriage that have been the object of intense study by theologians and biblical scholars are 1 Corinthians 7:10–16, Mark 10:2–12, Matthew 5:31–32, Matthew 19:-3–12, and Luke 16:18. The first tradition is that of Saint Paul. The earliest extant example of the Gospel genre is that of Mark. Matthew and Luke have been drawn independently from Mark and have also based their statements on a now lost collection of sayings called the Q Document. They have always been the focal point of intense study on the part of theologians and biblical scholars down through the ages and recently have unleashed a flood of literature. Because there is no unanimity of interpretation of these passages among the scholars, the Church has never attempted to define their sense.[7]

### 1 CORINTHIANS 7:10–16

A significant passage of the New Testament on marriage is Paul's discussion in 1 Corinthians 7:10–16. It is important for a number of reasons. It is chronologically the earliest witness of Jesus' words and the early Christian community's struggle with their meaning. It also points out the mutual obligation of both husband and wife. Finally, it addresses a pastoral problem in the expanding population of the early Christian community. It not only addresses the gentile Christians but also non-Christians, which leads to distinctions between what the Lord himself said and what Paul was asserting.

To those now married, however, I give this command (though it is not mine; it is the Lord's): a wife must not separate from her husband. If she does separate, she must either remain single or become reconciled to him again. Similarly, a husband must not divorce his wife.

As for the other matters, although I know of nothing the Lord has said, I say: If any brother has a wife who is an unbeliever but is willing to live with him, he must not divorce her. And if any woman has a husband who is an unbeliever but is willing to live with her, she must not divorce him. The unbelieving husband is consecrated by his believing wife; the unbelieving wife is consecrated by her believing husband. If it were otherwise, your children should be unclean; but as it is, they are holy.

If the unbeliever wishes to separate, however, let him do so. The believing husband or wife is not bound in such cases. God has called you to live in peace. Wife, how do you know that you will not save your husband; or you, husband, that you will not save your wife?

Apparently Paul is pointing out that there has to be authoritative adjustment and application of even the words of Jesus to the wide variety of human circumstances that go beyond the brief directives of the Lord. The bedrock of Paul's reasoning for making exceptions to Jesus' words is that this is necessary in order to maintain the very theme of the Lord's teaching—peace. He simply states "God has called you to live in peace." Paul seems quite confident that since the Spirit has come, he can understand many other things in the light of the Lord's direction. For two thousand years after Paul, the Church made exceptions to the Lord's own words based on this passage and called it the Pauline Privilege.

## MARK 10:2–12

The second writing came about twelve years later in a different part of the world when Mark was writing in Rome. Mark 10:2–12 has the key expression of Jesus' position on the indissolubility of marriage. The setting is a dispute the Pharisees were having among themselves and subsequently took to Jesus. Because of the teaching nature of the passage, the question asked, the Scripture referred to, the instruction given, the reactions of the listeners, and the repeat of the concluding statement, this pronouncement of Jesus is paramount above all the others.

Then some Pharisees came up and as a test began to ask him whether it was permissible for a husband to divorce his wife. In reply he said, "What command did Moses give you?" They answered, "Moses permitted divorce and the writing of a decree of divorce." But Jesus told them: "He wrote that commandment for you because of your stubbornness. At the beginning of creation God made them male and female; for this reason a man shall leave his father and mother and the two shall become as one. They are no longer two but one flesh. Therefore let no man separate what

God has joined." Back in the house again, the disciples began to question him about this. He told them, "Whoever divorces his wife and marries another commits adultery against her; and the woman who divorces her husband and marries another commits adultery."

Most Scripture scholars hold this to be the most explicit teaching of Jesus on the permanency of marriage. It is the first Gospel statement on the subject and the closest reference to the Q Document. In favor of the form critics and traditionalists, it is obvious that Mark makes an adaptation for his Western audience by having Jesus say the prohibition of divorce applies to women as well as to men. It was unthinkable for a woman to divorce her husband in Judaic culture. If Jesus had said that to the Pharisees, they would have laughed openly or discounted his whole teaching as one coming from an ignorant person; clearly that was Mark's addition.

The reason that Church authorities and scholars are confident of Jesus' unqualified prohibition of divorce and remarriage is that the three main sources, Mark, Q, and Paul's Letters, state this as his position. If the early Christians followed the directives of the Lord concerning the matter of divorce, they would certainly have stood out, for the Lord's position runs radically counter to the accepted practices of both Jewish and Greco-Roman societies. A very brief vignette following the parallel text in Matthew (19:3–12) points out how stunned the Jewish disciples were with Jesus' statements. They seemed to think that such a position was hopeless. "If that is the case between man and wife, it is better not to marry" (Matt. 19:10).

## MATTHEW 5:31–32 AND 19:3–12

Both Mark and Matthew place the Lord's teachings on divorce and remarriage in the bitter social and religious conflict of the time. In fact, both of these Evangelists explicitly state that the religious leaders made their inquiry to Jesus as a test. It is not without interest that both Gospel clauses that provide an exception to the rule of no divorce appear in Matthew who, unlike the other Evangelists, wrote for a predominately Jewish audience. The two passages are:

"It was also said, 'Whenever a man divorces his wife, he must give her a decree of divorce.' What I say to you is: everyone who divorces his wife—lewd conduct is a separate case—forces her to commit adultery. The man who marries a divorced woman likewise commits adultery."

(Matt. 5:31–32)

Some Pharisees came up to him and said, to test him, "May a man divorce his wife for any reason whatever?" He replied: "Have you not read that at the beginning the Creator made them male and female and declared, 'For this reason a man shall leave his father and mother and cling to his wife, and the two shall become as one'? Thus they are no longer two but one flesh. Therefore, let no man separate what God has joined." They said to him, "Then why did Moses command divorce and the promulgation of a divorce decree?" "Because of your stubbornness Moses let you divorce your wives," he replied: "but at the beginning it was not that way. I now say to you, whoever divorces his wife (lewd conduct is a separate case) and marries another commits adultery, and the man who marries a divorced woman commits adultery."

His disciples said to him, "If that is the case between man and wife, it is better not to marry." He said, "Not everyone can accept this teaching, only those to whom it is given to do so. Some men are incapable of sexual activity from birth; some have been deliberately made so; and some there are who have freely renounced sex for the sake of God's reign. Let him accept this teaching who can."

(Matt. 19:3–12)

The debate raging at the time Matthew wrote his Gospel was between the rabbinical schools of Shammai and Hillel. Both traditions were arguing over the meaning of the passage of Deuteronomy 24:1. This passage of the Old Testament states:

When a man, after marrying a woman and having relations with her, is later displeased with her because he finds in her something indecent, and therefore he writes out a bill of divorce and hands it to her, thus dismissing her from his house . . .

About a century before the time of Jesus, Rabbi Shammai held that "indecency" applied only to adultery. A contemporary, Rabbi Hillel, held that it applied not only to adultery but also to whatever caused the husband displeasure. Since an aspect of holiness among the rabbis was to constantly explore the meaning of the Torah, controversies such as this one were kept alive for centuries. If we were to adhere closely to the meaning of the text, Jesus in Matthew would be siding with the school of Shammai. These exception clauses, however, do not rest comfortably next to the more original texts of Mark and the Q Document. With far more humility than the schools of Shammai and Hillel of old, common Catholic and Protestant Scripture scholars openly admit the exception clause of Matthew is very confusing. Most would tend to translate the meaning of the New Testament term as some form of incest. Among believing Christians it would be rare to hear a priest or minister use a single act of adultery as a reason to divorce a spouse. In general, even the literalists are mute about Matthew's exception clause.[8] Without doubt, Matthew stands uncontested among Evangelists for causing the greatest amount of controversy down through the centuries with his exception clause. Literalists choose either Matthew or Mark; parallelists are stunned; form critics take votes on its meaning; and traditionalists have a field day.

However, while the controversial exception passage in Matthew 19:9 seems to draw excessive attention to itself, the following three verses go unnoticed. Yet in them the disciples seem to grasp clearly what Jesus is saying about the indissolubility of marriage. Apparently reflecting the marriage problems of their time, the disciples respond: "If that is the case . . . it is better not to marry." And Jesus, while not compromising his stated ideal about marriage, continues with his typical appreciation of people's varying abilities and his pastoral love when he says:

"Not everyone can accept this teaching, only those to whom it is given to do so. Some men are incapable of sexual activity from birth; some have been deliberately made so; and some there are who have freely renounced sex for the sake of God's reign. Let him accept this teaching who can"

(Matt. 19:11–12)

The passage seems to have Jesus implicitly saying, "I will accept people according to each one's capability."
Luke 16:18

The final main writing, by the Evangelist Luke, is a single verse, 18, contained in chapter 16 and constitutes the briefest statement of the five. It was probably written a half-century after the death of Jesus.

"Everyone who divorces his wife and marries another commits adultery. The man who marries a woman divorced from her husband likewise commits adultery."

### OTHER PASSAGES

There are two other scriptural references that do have a bearing on the subject of divorce and remarriage. One is the lengthy and loving description of Jesus' conversation with the Samaritan woman who had been married five times (John 4:7–30). The other is Ephesians 5:25–33. In this latter passage Paul introduces the concept of marriage as a reflection of Jesus' undying faithfulness to his church.

Husbands, love your wives, as Christ loved the church. He gave himself up for her to make her holy, purifying her in the bath of water by the power of the word, to present to himself a glorious church, holy and immaculate, without stain or wrinkle or anything of that sort. Husbands should love their wives as they do their own bodies. He who loves his wife loves himself. Observe that no one ever hates his own flesh; no, he nourishes it and takes care of it as Christ cares for the church—for we are members of his body.

"For this reason a man shall leave his father and mother, and shall cling to his wife, and the two shall be made into one."

This is a great foreshadowing; I mean that it refers to Christ and the church. In any case, each one should love his wife as he loves himself, the wife for her part showing respect for her husband.

This passage was to become the Achilles' heel of pastoral practice from the eleventh century on, because Roman Catholicism took this covenantal concept of Jesus and his church and made it a moral imperative for all Church marriages.

The equation spelled out in this passage is this: the relation of husband and wife is compared to the relation of Jesus and the Church. Since Jesus died for the Church (his people) and there were no exceptions to his faithfulness to it, every Christian marriage should be bound by the same quality of faithfulness. The severe appreciation of this equation maintains that once a marriage is proclaimed as Christian, there can never be another marriage because Jesus never chose another spouse.

The unmitigated application of this analogy to marriage is troublesome. People obviously do not imitate other areas of Jesus' life to perfection, and there is forgiveness for it. What makes divorce and remarriage the unforgivable sin? Matthew twice gives an exception to the rule. And the fact that remarriage in the Church was practiced for centuries indicates that there was an appreciation of the need to remarry in some instances. If Christians are strict in enforcing the Ephesian equation, there should be no second marriage even after the physical death of one's spouse because Jesus did not choose another spouse. In reality, following physical death, remarriage is permitted. The greatest question of all remains, is every marriage that takes place in church "Christian"?

A fascinating aspect of divorce and remarriage in Christian history is the expulsion or alienation of the divorced person from the local religious community. In many incidents in history, Christian communities have been cruel in dubbing the divorced person a sinner, when in fact, many divorced people have been sinned against. The main Scripture passages are directed primarily against remarriage, not divorce alone. Paul prohibits the very act of divorce alone. Even then, he does so with his exception.

In the first place the scriptural passages primarily point toward the prohibition of remarriage—"If anyone puts away his wife *and* marries another. . . . " Sin is principally incurred with the remarriage.

It is significant that Matthew is the only Evangelist who points out divorce alone as a sin. In Matthew 5:32, the author, writing for a Jewish population, states, ". . . but I say to you: Anyone who divorces his wife . . . makes her an adulteress." In Jesus' Jewish culture, a woman who was set aside in marriage could often only support herself by prostitution or, if she were fortunate, by remarriage. Women were totally dependent upon men. In most instances following divorce, a woman did not return to her original family. She had no other option but to support herself by being further used by men. Jesus was constantly emphasizing the dignity and rights of women. This is another case of his protest. The New Testament passages primarily point to sin in the remarriage, not the divorce. However, the passage in Matthew's Gospel reminds its readers that if an injustice is going to occur toward a spouse, especially a woman, then divorce alone could be a sin.

It becomes more puzzling to see Catholic pastoral practice toward divorced people in the light of Jesus' pastoral practice toward them. John is the only Evangelist of the four who does not give the words of Jesus on divorce and remarriage. Yet he outdistances the other three put together with his tender and loving story of the Lord's conversation with the Samaritan woman by the well (John 4:7–30). The story has many facets to it. Jesus' respect for this woman is overwhelming. He seems comfortable with the fact that she has been married five times before. He is not chiding; he is not demeaning. It is obvious that Jesus is aware of her having failed five times in marriage, but to him she is not a failure. It is to this half-breed (Samaritan) and woman that he speaks of the profound ideas of baptism, grace, the Kingdom, and redemption. It is to this five-times divorced person that he reveals the secret of his messiahship. With a marriage record like that and a lifestyle of open concubinage, it is highly improbable that she would have had any status in the town. Yet the Lord's honoring of her person and acknowledging her dignity gave her so much energy that she called the entire town out to meet the Lord. It is profoundly perplexing why this story is virtually always omitted from the discussion of the indissolubility of marriage and seems to have had little or no influence on the pastoral practice of Christian communities toward the divorced.

## BOUND/NOT BOUND

It should be highlighted that Jesus wasn't talking only about Christian marriage in his prohibition of divorce and remarriage. He was addressing all marriages. In fact he goes back to the creation and the institution of marriage in the beginning of humankind. This issue leads us into the question of sacramental marriage.

When Saint Paul mentions in his Corinthian Epistle (7:15) that the Christian partner who is "deserted" is "not bound," it is important to note that he is not talking sacramentally. That would be reading history backward to argue that the New Testament is even implicitly talking about the distinction between sacramental and nonsacramental marriage. This was articulated many centuries later in the theological development of the Church. Sacramental marriage came to mean the union of a baptized man and women capable of marrying each other. Such a couple wished to make a permanent promise to each other to make their love for each other and for Jesus Christ central in their lives. What is most significant is that the later Church was responsible for the distinction, not any divine law. Therefore if the Church was responsible, it is also empowered to modify that distinction if it would see fit to do so. In the next chapter it will be shown that during the entire first millennium the Church had exceptions to indissolubility. During the second millennium rigidity began to exclude them. What could it be for the third millennium?

It cannot be argued that the exception clauses of Matthew or Paul have to do with separation without the right to remarry. In the Jewish tradition it is expected that the male will remarry after divorce. If the context of Matthew is a Jewish-Christian one, making an exception is simply meaningless if there is no remarriage. In the exception passage of Paul's Letter to the Corinthians, he explicitly rules out remarriage in the first case he deals with—that of the Christian partner initiating separation. It is probably also true that, given his eschatalogical perspective, Paul would dissuade the divorced Christian partner of a mixed marriage from remarrying. At the same time he makes it unequivocally clear in the same context (chap. 7) that those who are free, that is, widows and those who have never been married, do no wrong, even in the situation of a proximate eschatological expectation, if they choose to remain unmarried. As a consequence it is difficult to imagine him holding an unexpressed reservation about remarriage for the victims of a broken marriage he calls "not bound."9

## MARRIAGE: THE SIGN OF UNION OF CHRIST AND THE CHURCH

Today the Catholic Church singles out the fifth chapter of Ephesians as the most important concerning marriage. Interestingly enough this passage was not effectively referred to by the Church for the first eleven hundred years. In fact it is not one of the four passages that refers to Jesus' own words on divorce and remarriage. After the twelfth century A.D., the Church took Saint Paul's Letter to the Ephesians and referred to marriage as a sign of Christ's covenant with the church. In the fifth chapter of this Letter Saint Paul refers to the description of the creation of marriage in the book of Genesis (Gen. 1:24): "That is why a man leaves his father and his mother and clings to this wife, and the two of them become one body." In both Luke and Matthew Jesus also refers to this passage in his dispute with the Pharisees. But Paul goes on in verse 32, however, to add the words, "This is a great foreshadowing: I mean it refers to Christ and the Church." In this critical passage Paul gives the premise for marriages of the New Testament to be the sign of the covenant of Christ and the Church.

There is a very close similarity between the passage of the Old Testament in Hosea and the passage of the New Testament in Ephesians. In the Old Testament, Hosea is asked to retain his unfaithful wife just as Yahweh, who is espoused to the people, keeps them regardless of their unfaithfulness. So, also in Saint Paul's Letter to the Ephesians in the New Testament, marriage is to be the sign of Christ's faithfulness to his Church regardless of the status of its faithfulness.

The permanent marriage appears in the Old Testament as the ideal: it reflects the union of Yahweh and his people. In the New Testament, the demand is that every marriage reflect the union of Christ and his people. The conclusion then is that in Old Testament times and the first eleven hundred years after Jesus' death, if a marriage failed there was sadness because the ideal was not achieved. After the thirteenth century, if a marriage failed, there was sin because the command was broken.

Religiously, then, the intensity of pain concerning divorce and remarriage reached a zenith when the Church's position evolved from an ideal to a command. So, too, the pain could be lessened if the process were reversed.

When we look at all that was said and written by saints and scholars, in times past and times present, the overwhelming conclusion is there is not the least semblance of unanimity about the interpretation of Scripture's passages on divorce and remarriage. So, among religious people the merciful continue to be kind and the severe continue to be binding. The Church too is faced with this choice!

# 3. History: How Church Teaching and Practice Have Varied and Changed

## SPIRIT OR LAW?

In a fascinating way Jesus speaks in parables and stories that can be understood by people of all cultures and times. His ideals are sublime. They appeal to love, kindness, and the perfection of the human, now singularly enlightened by the divine. Noticeably absent in his legacy are training manuals, codes, or books of rules and regulations. Love laces his teachings. People of goodwill are to fulfill his teachings in a manner inspired by the Spirit. The Spirit is present all days till the end of time. This presence is also a source of divine revelation called tradition.

It is said that people who stand on the shoulders of those who have gone before them will be giants. A Church with two thousand years of experience and celebration of the spirit of Jesus could be a giant in the pastoral care of the divorced; it should never lock this storehouse of experience. The New Pentecost, Vatican II, made Catholics acutely aware of this. It pointed out that many of the religious practices and customs Catholics presumed were formulated from the beginning were less than a century old. Some of these religious practices actually developed as a reaction to heresies and for that reason reeked of fear.

One advantage of studying the traditions of the Church is that history is impartial. It has no vested interests. Studying history expands our vision and shows us people enlightened as well as limited by their particular cultures.

The parade of Christian history seems to reflect the long-standing struggle between Church members who insist on the ideal and those ministering to the broken, between those who are the "light of the world" and those who are the sick and the poor. Church legislation insists upon the ideal while Church practice ministers to those who cannot keep it.

## DIFFERENT CHURCH PERSPECTIVES

There are three perspectives that readers of marriage history must keep in mind. First, the Church is comprised of East and West. The Eastern tradition, sometimes called the Oriental or Byzantine tradition, is distinctly different from the Western life perspective. People from the Eastern tradition often tell their story in myth and imagery. They tend to have more of a world view, a holistic approach to life's problems and events. The Western perspective is more chronological, exact, and legalistic. Jesus was of the Eastern culture, not the Western. The "Roman" Church often forgets this.

Second, there has never been any uniform religious practice demanded by Church legislation for all Catholics. Church laws and practices differ from place to place and from age to age. Local councils and senates have in the past attempted to pull things together, but invasions, migrations, plagues, general disorder, and society in general made it hard for the Church to legislate at all, much less communicate that legislation. Since Jesus left no "how-to" instructions for the sacraments, the early Christians used earlier religious practices and simply "baptized" them or gave them Christian meaning. The very large Church population in Africa viewed Christianity quite differently from the converted Germanic tribes.

Third, Western readers of history often expect to find perfect chronology and clear, linear development of events. Yet sometimes a half century passed before there was any contact between the various early Christian communities. Communication was difficult. As a result, Church practices, devotions, and even beliefs grew independently of one another even though they may have been similar in origin.

Seen in this light, Church tradition is a collage of insights and practices given unity (not uniformity) by the one Spirit. For the rigid, it's frustrating; for the imaginative, it's fascinating. History can truly kill the letter-of-the-law people; to those of the Spirit, it can give life.

Caution must be taken in reading the history of the first thousand years of the Christian era. It is sketchy; documentation is not plentiful. What we have leaves much to be desired for the inquisitive mind. With these things in mind, we begin our journey through the history of the Catholic Church's handling of divorce and remarriage.

## PRE-CHRISTIAN HISTORY OF MARRIAGE

In prehistoric and ancient cultures, marriage was the natural sign for the unity of man and woman, family and tribe. It was part of the network of making clear the relationships that bound people together in kinship and friendship. Marriage customs and ceremonies took a variety of forms in different parts of the world at different times and depended on such things as occupation and social position. Tribal ceremonies revealed whether the marriages were permanent or temporary, headed by men or women, or joined clans or individuals. They defined relationships between the sexes, established rights and responsibilities for parents and offspring, and provided for cohesiveness and continuity in the society. Marriage was one way of ritualizing a community identity whether it was nomadic or sedentary in its lifestyle, hunting or farming for its existence, or tribal or urbanized in its organization.

Sociological research over the years has repeatedly confirmed the fact that no tribe is without an "altar", that is, a God-consciousness. So it is not surprising that an important tribal ceremony like marriage would be replete with religious symbolism.[10]

Since the majority of the people who became Christian in the early centuries were adults, the concept of marriage as sacred was drawn from what was accepted everywhere. Baptism merely sealed that marriage in Christ Jesus. The concept of marriage as a sacrament and separate ceremony was foreign to them. This practice did not surface until the twelfth century.

Marriage ceremonies in both the Jewish and Greco-Roman traditions were richly religious without being associated with synagogue or temple. The Jewish wedding lasted a week. All of it was deemed religious, but the core of the liturgical part of the celebration was a series of seven benedictions read by the father of the groom.

Roman law had no special specific form of manifesting marital consent, therefore the Jews as well as other subjugated people were allowed to keep or develop their own ceremonial rites of marriage or have none at all. By far the most important figures at the time of the marriage ceremony were the fathers of the bride and groom. For the most part they were the ones who made the contract in the first place. It was the father of the groom who presided at the wedding. Since the peoples of the Roman Empire did not have priest, priestess, or rabbi at the marriage rites, neither did the Christians have bishop or priest present.[11]

Many of our wedding practices today have lost their original meaning for us. The carrying of the bride across the threshold originally signified bringing her into the domain of the gods of her new household. This brought about unity of religion in the family. Adultery was the number one sin. Why? Because the child would be the offspring of two different family religions and thus would be torn in his or her allegiance to two different sets of gods.

The sharing of the wedding cake was a sharing of communion between the marriage partners and the gods of the household. The wedding ring traditionally meant intimacy of heart which, for most couples, had a religious connotation along with its emotional one. The orgasm of marital sexual love was often seen as a prelude to the ecstasy of the heavens and the resulting conception a sharing in the creative power of the god of life. The throwing of seed (rice) was a fertility rite showering blessing upon the couple for child-bearing. Much later, by and large such practices for converts to Christianity were easily made into liturgical ceremonies expressing the ideals of Jesus concerning marriage.

## CHRISTIAN HISTORY

Generally speaking, Christians were married in accordance with the customs of the land. There were no separate Christian ceremonies at all. The Roman government provided a wide framework of civil laws regulating marriage. Quite obviously, it never entered the Christian Roman citizen's mind to create new marriage rituals or practices since what they had sufficed. Different rituals would have made Christians more distinct and even more of a target during the off-and-on persecutions in the early centuries.

Since marriage customs varied, there was no agreement on how or when the transition from man and woman to husband and wife actually took place. Some saw the marriage consummated by the contract made by the parents, the contract between the couple themselves, the purchase of the bride by the groom, the giving of the rings, the signing of a document, the taking the bride into the new home, or the first act of intercourse. Others saw it as the whole series of actions, including all the wedding preparations. For others merely living together was sufficient. Private agreements of marriage were also used by the early Christians because that, too, was a practice of their counterparts. Among the Germanic tribes, not even mutual consent was necessary. Gifts and money were exchanged as a deed of purchase; a marriage document was drawn up and a ring given to symbolize the contract.

Women in both the Eastern and Western cultures did not have a chance for equal rights in the patriarchal structure, for only men had legal rights. "Husband" meant owner, and so he possessed the body and the property of his wife as well as his children. This concept began to change as Rome extended its empire throughout Italy and into the Mediterranean area. Men were gone for long periods of time and sometimes never returned home. Women learned to manage the family affairs and the courts eventually honored their decisions by law. As children matured to adulthood, they began to make their own decisions including their marital selections. Older tribal or family values were replaced by more nationalistic ones, and the individual religions of the hearth and home gave way to an imperial religion of glory and gods. The wedding ceremonial customs still continued throughout the early centuries of the Roman Empire but no doubt lost the early intensity of their religious meaning. Later the Roman priest was sometimes invited to the wedding to offer sacrifice to the gods or to bring down the protection of the divine on the couple. It is probable that the early Christians found this practice acceptable as well.

In the West, divorce was considered a private affair that could be initiated and carried out by either partner. It did not require approval of the civil authority or the judgment of any court.

Marriage, both in the East and the West, was looked on by the State and therefore the Church as any other contract. If the marriage failed, it was addressed like any other failure, like stealing, avoiding serving in the army, or even denying the faith. Divorce and remarriage as the unforgivable sin does not appear until the eleventh century. For centuries upon centuries, Christians treated divorce like any other failure or sin—with sadness, with a time of penance and prayer, forgiveness, and the ability to remarry.

The first witnesses to listen to as we begin the journey through the pages of Church history, are the fathers of the church, the great writers in the early church after the time of the apostles. Their theological speculation spans from about A.D. 100 to 700. They had a powerful influence on the development of Christian ideals and thought in the early centuries, for they both recorded theology and fashioned it. Of particular interest is that some of these early fathers were married men themselves.

### THE INFANCY YEARS

It seems rather evident that the early writers looked upon the Gospel statements of Jesus as an ideal rather than a moral imperative. In their mind there was no question that Jesus affirmed the permanency of marriage. We have already mentioned the exception clauses of Saint Paul, in about A.D. 57, and Saint Matthew, writing about A.D. 85. The first known canonical writer to follow their lead was the Shepherd of Hermas in the year 140. For certain reasons he allows divorce but does not favor a second marriage.

Around A.D. 110 in a letter to Polycarp, Ignatius of Antioch wrote that "those who are married should be united with the consent of their bishop, to be sure that they are marrying according to the Lord and not to satisfy their lust."[12] It should be noted that even here "consent of the bishop" does not necessarily refer to a blessing or even to a church ceremony, but more to the close relationship maintained between the early Christian communities and their religious leaders. In A.D. 200 Tertullian, in letters to his wife, speaks of marriage "sealed by a church blessing."

### CAMELOT

The Greeks and the Romans had many philosophies about the meaning of marriage in which it ranged from the sacred to the profane. Christians during this time were not free from this controversy. In A.D. 210 Clement of Alexandria defended the sacredness of marriage against those who considered it evil, although he did not mention divorce. A contemporary theologian, Origen, also picked up his pen in defense of the holiness of marriage, though today's theology would say his defense of marriage was so qualified as to be counterproductive. Still, at that time it was a step forward.

Origen chided the religious leaders of his day for acting "outside of holy Scripture" by allowing divorced women to remarry while their husbands were still living. At the same time he conceded to the reasonableness of remarriage lest its prohibition cause men and women to live together without marriage. This acknowledgment points out that it was becoming common in the Christian communities to interpret Saint Matthew's exception clause (5:32; 19:9) as condoning divorce in the case of adultery and allowing the man to remarry. Since the Gospels were clear in forbidding an adulterous wife from remarrying but seemed ambiguous about her husband, men were not considered acting "outside of holy Scripture."[13]

Origen wrote in a Palestinian area. As an example of how the early Christian communities developed separately without any uniformity, eighty years later, in 300, the Council of Elvira in Spain restricted women's right to divorce. The Council of Arles in France followed the same prejudice by allowing the husband to divorce but not the wife. It must be remembered that the Roman law during this time gave husbands and wives equal privileges. In this regard, the Church was more prejudiced than the empire. On the other hand, the early Christian church granted equality between men and women in two aspects: one was by allowing both civil defiance; the other was in social attitude.

One of the most significant differences about marriage among the early Christians was that they ignored the imperial law forbidding marriage between citizens and slaves or foreigners. Roman law allowed concubinage in this regard, but not marriage. Marriage would legitimate the children and give them a right to citizenship and inheritance; concubinage would not. From the beginning Christians allowed slaves and citizens to marry. Pope Callistus I (A.D. 217–222) was criticized by the Christian writer Hippolytus for violating civil law by allowing Christian women citizens to marry freed men, even slaves. This was the first appearance in Christian history of "the marriage of conscience," a marriage kept secret from civil authorities in violation of the law. The conduct of Pope Callistus is the oldest solid evidence we have of effective episcopal intervention in Christian marriages.

The second major difference between Christians and the Romans was one of attitude. Christians had a different sexual attitude toward women. The words of Jesus were normative for the Christian man: "but I say to you, he who even looks at a woman to lust after her has already committed adultery with her in his heart" (Matt. 5:28). A man who became a Christian knew this and presumably accepted it when he converted because he wanted to live in such a moral climate. He knew the Christian demand that wives be cherished and that the same moral obligations bind husbands and wives equally. This was in stark contrast to the sexual mores of Roman men. For them wife stealing and wife trading were common enterprises. A visit to the neighborhood brothel was almost as common as a business lunch today.[14]

It was at this time (A.D. 313) that the emperor Constantine allowed religious freedom for Christians. The practice of the empire was to give attention to both the man and the woman in a divorce. As a consequence, the prevailing practice of the early Church for centuries to come was to allow divorce and remarriage. For the next seven hundred years, though councils of the Church, individual theologians, and even emperors emphasized the higher standard of no divorce and remarriage, the practice of the Church was to accept it. Seeing the necessity in some marriages for separation and divorce, Emperor Constantine in 331 tightened up Roman law on allowing husbands and wives mutually consenting to divorce in order to give strength to the permanency of marriage.

The first Christian churchman to write that no marriage should be dissolved for any reason and insist that not even men had the right to remarry as long as their first wives were alive was Ambrose, bishop of Milan, around A.D. 380. Ambrose did not even allow divorce and remarriage in the case of adultery. He was alone in holding this position; divorce and remarriage continued in the Church. However Ambrose's unmitigated position had an influence on the writings of his protégé, Saint Augustine, who in turn had the greatest influence on scholars in the early Middle Ages.[15]

Across the Aegean, Basil of Caesarea, in A.D. 375, commented on the double standard prevailing in the East that allowed men to remarry but not women, and at the beginning of the fifth century

Saint Augustine of Hippo recommended the tightening up of Christian moral teachings. Augustine was the principal spokesman for the large Christian population in Africa. Through the power of his personality he persuaded the Council of Carthage to forbid remarriage after divorce. Yet this proclamation yielded without contest within fifty years to Emperor Theodosius II's proclamation expanding the list of legitimate grounds for leaving one's spouse and including the option to remarry. It was not legal for a woman to divorce a husband for adultery. The legitimate grounds for leaving one's spouse included robbery, kidnapping, treason, and a wide variety of other serious crimes.

This same kind of understanding was reflected by the bishops of the East. In general they took the term *porneia* ("indecency") in Saint Matthew's exception clause to mean any kind of gross immorality. Veering away from the double standard that had existed in the East for such a long time, they gave wives similar privileges as husbands in divorcing for immorality or lewd conduct. It might also be said that in spite of Theodosius' law against consensual divorces, later emperors again permitted it.

### The Huns Are Coming

Roughly from 400 to 700 boundaries in Europe changed frequently as the Roman Empire crumbled into smaller kingdoms. Lands were devastated by the migration of the Huns. Towns were taken and lost many times. In the outlying areas Christianity was even obliterated. Documentation of marriage and divorce, as of other social events, was virtually nil. Without doubt Christians practiced marriage, divorce, and remarriage according to the sociopolitical directives of whatever area they were in. With such general political upheaval the theology of marriage was not an interesting topic of discussion. The Catholic Church in the Byzantine world of the East was more fortunate.

Monumental in the history of the Church's practice of divorce and remarriage is the brilliant code of the emperor Justinian in the year A.D. 550. This energetic, powerful, and deeply religious man was emperor from 527 to 565. His great aim was to unite the East and the West in a harmonious empire. Justinian even called the Church Council of Constantinople (A.D. 553) to help a less gifted pope deal with the rising heresy of Nestorius and the constant struggle between the East and the West. In his usual reconciling and sensitive manner, Justinian held up permanent marriage as the ideal. The law provided practical norms for those who could not or would not live up to it. Both husband and wife had nearly equal grounds for divorce. The children of a dissolved marriage remained the responsibility of one or the other parent or both. The traditional grounds for one-sided divorce were affirmed. Adding to the already existing grounds for divorce were impotence, absence due to slavery, and the termination of the marriage by entering religious life. This code held sway in both the East and the West.

The oldest evidence of a Christian marriage solemnized by an officiating bishop or priest dates from the fourth century. Since the priests themselves married at this time, the obligation to marry in the Church applied only to them; it was considered a privilege for the laity. But Church weddings were not permitted for people whose lives were scandalous or for second marriages.[16] Just before the Council of Constantinople, there began a custom in Greece and Asia Minor of the priest taking a more active part in the wedding ceremonies of the laity. At first he merely blessed them; then as time went on, he joined their hands and/or he put the garland of unity around them. For the next century and a half this was the practice in this area of Christendom; it later became part of the liturgy. Even this, however, did not mean that the Church was replacing the state in joining couples in marriage.

This "churching of marriages" spread to the West during the seventh and eighth centuries. Gradually the popularity of using the church instead of the home led to civil legislation allowing the wedding ceremony to be legally valid when performed by a priest. The joining of two people in a Christian sacramental marriage first appears at this time in the Greek Church of the East. Two centuries later, with far less theological prompting, in the West the priest was encouraged to perform the marriage on behalf of the state. This took place when civil governments so disintegrated that the clergy were generally the only qualified people to take care of matters like marriage.

While the power of the Church to perform marriages grew steadily, its attitude toward remarriage after divorce was erratic, ranging from extreme strictness to extreme laxness. Here again there was a wide gap between Church proclamations and Church practice. For this reason, Church historians simply state that the Church permitted remarriage during the first millennium.

In Spain, the Third and Fourth Councils of Toledo in A.D. 589 and 633 invoked the Pauline Privilege and allowed Christian converts from Judaism to remarry. An Irish penitential book written in the seventh century directed that if one allowed one's spouse to enter the service of God in a monastery or convent, the one was free to remarry.[17] The penitential of Theodore, archbishop of Canterbury, in the same century allowed a husband to divorce an adulterous wife and remarry. The wife in that case could also remarry after doing penance for five years. A man who was deserted by his wife could remarry after two years provided he had his bishop's consent. A woman whose husband was imprisoned for a serious crime could remarry, but only with the bishop's consent. A man whose wife was abducted by an enemy could remarry, and if she later returned, she could also remarry. Freed slaves who could not purchase their spouse's freedom were allowed to marry other free persons. Penitential books from other parts of the continent had similar provisions, and although the Council of Hereford in England advised against remarriage, it did not forbid it.

## CATHOLICISM BEGINNING TO RECOVER

True to this uneven pattern, in A.D. 752 the Council of Verberie enacted legislation that allowed both men and women to remarry if their spouses committed adultery with a relative, yet it prohibited the adulterers from remarrying. It also permitted a man to divorce and remarry if his wife plotted to kill him, or if he had to leave his homeland permanently and his wife refused to go with him. In 826, Pope Gregory II advised Boniface, the missionary bishop of Germany, that if a wife was too sick to perform her wifely duties, it was best that her husband practice continence, but if this were impossible he might have another wife provided he took care of the first one. Boniface recognized desertion as grounds for divorce, as well as adultery and entrance into a convent or monastery. Yet at the same time the popes of this period protested against what they considered to be unlawful divorces, and the Italian Council of Friuli in A.D. 791 strictly forbade divorced men to remarry even if their wives had been unfaithful.[18]

## LET'S GET SOME LAWS

The tug-of-war between Church pronouncements and practice continued and even intensified in the ninth century. At the beginning of this century the Church in northern Europe became more stringent under the impetus of ecclesiastical reform. At the Council of Paris, in A.D. 829, the bishops decreed that divorced persons of both sexes could not remarry even if the divorce had been granted for adultery. Several other councils in Italy and Germany passed similar prohibitions. At the same time popes and local councils continued to allow divorce and remarriage for certain reasons, especially adultery and entering religious life.

Confusion mounted to a crescendo when the missionaries in the Balkans, caught between the East and the West, wondered about the Greek Church's contention that Christian marriages were not valid unless they were performed and blessed by a priest. In 866 the ruling pontiff, Nicholas I, rocked the Eastern Church by stating that a marriage was legal and binding even without any public or liturgical ceremony. The marriage became valid at the moment of the consent of the two espousing partners. All other celebrations counted for nothing if this consent was not present.[19]

This proclamation of Pope Nicholas I reflected and encouraged the see-saw trend in the European Church. After it divorce regulations in the northern European Church became more stringent, then during the ninth and early part of the tenth century, relaxed again. In the next two centuries the councils of Bourges, Worms, and Tours again allowed remarriage in cases of adultery or desertion.[20]

## THE CHURCH IS BOSS—MORE LAWS

By the year 1000 all marriages in Europe effectively came under the jurisdiction of the Church. This was not opposed by the civil governments since they were, for the most part, in disarray; in many areas the civil functions of society were taken care of by the clergy. Since it had jurisdiction, the Church had to make rules about marriage that could be used in permitting or prohibiting remarriage.

Since there was nothing in Scripture as to when the marriage actually began, great theologians in the halls of learning argued excitedly as to whether the marriage took place at the time of consent, in the ceremony, or with the first act of intercourse. Obviously this had serious implications with regard to divorce and remarriage. Many things could happen between the time of apparent consent for marriage, the wedding ceremony, and the first act of intercourse. The two groups that carried the debate to its conclusion were the canonists of the University of Bologna and the theologians of the University of Paris.

A beacon of light in this controversy was Hugh of St. Victor of the University of Paris. He was the first Christian thinker since Augustine to present a fresh approach to the nature of marriage and when it was consummated. The summary of his work was published between 1130 and 1143.[21] For Hugh of St. Victor marriage took place when the spiritual relationship of the two spouses was present. This relationship was the reflection of God's own presence among his people and especially Jesus' presence in the Church. Because of the profound nature of this relationship, Christian marriage was not simply something sacred, which was held in primitive cultures, but a sacrament, which could be achieved only in Jesus Christ. By employing this spiritual insight he avoided getting mixed up in the mechanics of when consummation took place. The sacred relationship between two Christian people was the reflection of that of Christ with his Church, and that was a sacrament. For Hugh of St. Victor it did not matter whether a couple could have intercourse or not; what mattered was their love for each other. Through his teaching and that of his followers at the University of Paris, marriage took its place among the sacraments of the Church. On the basis of this concept there developed an even greater reservation concerning remarriage after divorce. As spiritually enlightened as Hugh of St. Victor was, even his concepts would not escape being translated into legalistic doctrine.

In A.D. 1150 Pope Alexander III taught that the marriage was ratified after its consummation in the first act of intercourse. The effects of this decision would likewise be felt all the way down to the present. From this time on, the marriage bond was considered indissoluble not only as a Christian ideal but also as a rule of law. In order for a Catholic to divorce and remarry, he or she would have to establish that consummation did not take place or use some other canonical, acceptable reason. In 1184 an official body of the Church, the Synod of Verona, for the first time in history proclaimed marriage as a sacrament.

## AND MORE LAWS

About a century later Saint Thomas Aquinas (d. 1274) and other theologians returned to the position that mutual consent established the marriage. The official language of the Church also began to refer to marriage as a "contract." The very word itself strongly implies legalism, which pervaded the ecclesiastical pronouncements on marriage for the next seven hundred years. The act of lovemaking was referred to as "rendering the debt." The biological act of intercourse sealed or consummated the marriage. No matter whether there was sin or pain in the marriage, couples had to "lie in the bed they made" and were denied any other options. For the next seven centuries virtually no new or different theology would be written about marriage.

Some of the reasons the sacrament of marriage was turned into legalistic doctrine were these. Marriage existed from the beginning of time, so it was not uniquely Christian. The history of marriage was replete with codes, rituals, and customs. Christian marriage had to identify itself in accord with or opposition to what preceded it. Marriages were often a part of treaties between countries and involved financial arrangements. Marriage was often taken as an arrangement in which something bought and sold.

The overwhelming factor, however, was that it was the only sacrament involving sex at a time when sex was suspect. During the second millennium a vast amount of systematic and ascetical theology was written by celibates. It is not accidental that most writings about marriage, then, were legalistic and theoretical, and virginity was held in higher esteem than marriage throughout the Middle Ages. Sexual desires were viewed as dangerous and sinful. Saint Paul's distaste for marriage was pointed out: he thought it better to remain single, although he conceded it was "better to marry than to burn."

This fear of sex, even within marriage, was reflected in many Church customs. In some places couples were encouraged to abstain from intercourse for the first three days after the wedding out of "respect" for each other and the blessing of the Church. In other places the custom of not going to Communion for a full month after the wedding prevailed because of the "impurity" from intercourse. Very often abstinence from intercourse for months and even years was done as penance. It was often implied that "the stain of original sin" was passed from person to person because of the manner in which each one was conceived.

Through Hugh of St. Victor the writings of Saint Augustine once more surfaced. Augustine had a broad concept of sacrament. In fact, he had fifty-nine sacraments. Hugh of Saint Victor developed marriage into a sacramental appreciation that was so profound it would take its place among the seven sacraments. His concept of marriage as a sacrament, a sign of union between Christ and his Church, did not mesh with the prevailing negative concept of sexuality. It was here in the thirteenth century, amidst this strange brew of theories, proclamations, and circumstances, that marriage as it reflected the loving union between Christ and his Church was changed from an invitation to holiness to a command binding two to its fulfillment under pain of sin.

Every marriage was seen as a contract reflecting the union of Christ and his church and was, therefore, irrevocable. If it were revocable, they reasoned, Christians might get the idea that the Savior was not faithful to his people. Perhaps if a healthier concept of sexuality had prevailed, the entire concept of marriage would have evolved as an invitation for couples to reflect the loving, intimate, ecstasy-filled relationship of Christ with his people. Like all other calls to holiness, it would have been an invitation, not a demand.

The very ones who fashioned this harsh and rigorous theology on marriage were too close to the issue to see their own injustice, an injustice that was to cause pain and "sin" for married couples for the next seven centuries. It is ironic that the men in orders who wrote this theology looked upon their own lifestyle as a way of perfection, a process, an invitation to holiness not binding under pain of sin, yet decreed the opposite for those who chose marriage and failed.

It was in the thirteenth century, the greatest era of religious theologians, that all Church marriages became the sign of Jesus' faithful love for the church. In the centuries to follow, churchmen developed the varied judicial aspects of the marital contract; its theology would be virtually untouched. One churchman, however, the Franciscan John Duns Scotus (d. 1308), wrote that marital intercourse could be for mutual love, for protecting the marriage bond, and not just for begetting children. Three centuries later other churchmen would finally concede that this is one of the ends of marriage. Scotus also held that the married couple and not the priest were the ministers of their sacrament.

### And a Few More Laws

In the West, from 1300 until the present, because of the binding force of the marital contract, separation was sometimes permitted for unfaithfulness, but divorce was not an option. Remarriage was gravely sinful and even at times resulted in excommunication. Over these centuries history reveals few exceptions to the Church's stand in this matter. These exceptions were usually granted to those of noble birth. Even though these annulments, as they were called, were granted for canonical reasons, it was often said that the Church treated the marriage as though it never existed. This ecclesiastical position caused some bitter fights with civil courts and some very damaging misconceptions people of the present era are still laboring under.

### Don't Think, Obey

At the time of the Reformation, the Catholic Church was attacked for its eccentric legalism; laws often seemed arbitrary, written to favor those with power or money, or derived from the Church-state conflict. Although Luther, Calvin, and other Protestant religious leaders who did not accept marriage as a sacrament were nevertheless opposed to divorce, they became much more lenient in dealing with human failure in marriage. They observed that even in Scripture there were exceptions to the rule prohibiting divorce. Luther extended the Pauline exception to include marriages in which one party became an unbeliever in one way or another.

### *The Council of Trent*

Bishops and theologians met at Trent beginning in 1545 in solemn council to attempt to unify and strengthen Catholic teaching. The question of marriage was not taken up until the last session in

1563. After months of lengthy speeches and reports, the council solemnly declared that marriage was a sacrament in the Catholic Church.

The council also delved into the question of the Church's legal authority over marriage. To that date, there had been no fundamental declaration by the Church concerning the basis of this power; it had simply evolved. The council debate was prolonged by a large bloc of bishops who refused to accept a one-sided document favoring almost exclusive Church control over marriage. In the document little power was left to the civil government. Theologians were called in and argued that the Church had competency only over marriage as a sacrament, while marriage as a contract should rest in the hands of the civil government. The bishops of Trent went on to assert, however, that the Church had the right to legislate regarding marriages for Catholics.

For the first time, the bishops insisted that all Catholics be married in the presence of a priest and two witnesses or the marriage would not be valid. Clandestine marriages were ruled out and became sinful. The bishops said nothing about the rights of the state. This left the door open for further study and further difficulties. What if the marriage law of the Church and that of the state contradicted one another? In spite of all the problems and unanswered questions, all Catholic marriages were now clearly under the control of the Church. This view still exists today.

To this doctrinal statement the bishops then added a series of canons condemning as heresy any opposition to the following statements: that marriage is a sacrament instituted by Christ that gives grace; that the Church has the power to regulate who can and cannot legally marry and to grant dispensations from these regulations; that ecclesiastical courts can annul unconsummated marriages and render judgments about other marriage cases; and that the Church is right in teaching that the marriage bond cannot be dissolved for any reason including adultery, and in forbidding remarriage, and in permitting spouses to legally separate without remarrying.[22]

## Church and State

Because of the division among Christian churches, the civil authorities gained steadily in the performance and legislation of marriages. Sometimes Catholic couples reached a compromise by getting married first by the state, then by the Church in the presence of a priest. However some civil governments in Protestant states ignored Catholic laws and demanded that marriage be contracted only by state laws. How were Catholic couples to square their consciences with secular realities? This problem reached its zenith when the Napoleonic code demanded that all weddings take place before civil authorities.

Some Catholic theologians found difficulty with the view that the state controlled marriage as a contract while the Church controlled it as a sacrament. They argued that the contract and sacrament were one and the same thing. In this view, only the unbaptized and Protestants were under civil control. Obviously this thinking was not popular with Protestant governments. The situation was all the more confusing for an increasing number of mixed marriages between Catholic and non-Catholic partners. The French Revolution further eroded the authority of the Church on marriage. In their search for freedom and equality, the revolutionaries demanded freedom from all religious marriage laws.

The woes of the Catholic Church brought on by its extensive legalism were not over. In the mid-1800s Pope Pius IX conceded to the sacramentality of non-Catholic Christians baptized marriages in their own denominations. However, the Church would not process a divorced Protestant's marriage for annulment claiming that it did not have jurisdiction over it. This catch-22 for Catholics wanting to marry divorced Protestants was acutely agonizing as divorce became more and more prevalent. The Catholic Church had legislated itself into a corner. Who gave it the privilege of making theological determinations on other Christians' marriages? If it were going to assume such a position, why didn't it also assume the care of those marriages?

## The Church in the Twentieth Century

Improved means of communication in the twentieth century brought a flood of burning questions about marriage to the courts of Rome. People of the Western world seemed tired of intellectual absolutism and tended toward existential philosophies enlightened by humanistic and holistic views of life. Even the attempt to establish a League of Nations after World War I pointed to the fact that all people belong first to the a human family, then to individual nations. The social sciences, psychology in particular, began to challenge the easy answers of the Church about complex human conditions. In many schools of Catholic theology there was a growing resentment against the legal, biological, and chemical approach to marriage that the Church seemed to reflect in its laws. To many in the world of study, the Church resembled a medieval knight protected by its armor of legalism plowing through a forest of human problems.

The simple legal decisions the Church faced were unbelievably complicated by the lack of a code of canon law, which was not formulated until 1917. In an ordinary legal problem, several Church scholars had to peruse many volumes of previous Church decisions and council pronouncements to arrive at an answer. To modern thinkers this was medieval and preposterous. To those of simple belief, such a process was holy because it was the way it had always been done.

On October 11, 1962, an unlikely looking messenger in the person of Pope John XXIII said to the very tired knight in legal armor, *aggiornamento*, "rise up and come out." Although opposed by staunch Church hierarchy, this very human and humorous pope called the Second Vatican Council to order. Then he stunned the world by apologizing to both Protestants and Jews for the sins that Catholics had committed against them. At the same time he chided the prophets of doom of the Church who maintained that it was not proper to admit to the sins of the Catholic ecclesiastical structure. And so the council began.

Like the proverbial crab that goes wild with pain when it grows and cracks its shell exposing itself to the brine of the sea, so the Church writhed with pain as its legalistic armor yielded to pronouncements that freed people rather than bound them. On December 7, 1965, in the final council event at Saint Peter's in Rome, the constitution "The Church and the Modern World" was promulgated. The problems of marriage and family were addressed. Noticeable in this document is the emphasis on a more personal perspective toward human relationships, sexuality, and marriage. It avoids speaking of marriage as a legal bond and refers to it in sociological, personal, and biblical terms. It enshrines marriage in both a social and divine setting and refers to it as an agreement between persons, an intimate partnership, a union in love, a community, and a covenant.

The decree "Apostolate of the Laity" from the council gave a broader meaning to the sacramentality of marriage. It encourages Christian couples to be signs to each other, their children, and the world of the love God has for his people and Christ has for the Church. The tone, however, seems to indicate this as an ideal to be approached by those couples who grasp the nature of the sacred in their marriages, rather than a rigid demand for all.

And in the recent promulgation of canon law on November 27, 1983, the Church yielded to social reality by recognizing that people who were married civilly may have acquired responsibilities. A Catholic married outside the Church can no longer dispense with that marriage by saying "it doesn't count" or avoid consequences that may include alimony, child support, or restitution of property. And the new code explicitly acknowledges the legitimacy of the children from either valid or putative (commonly accepted) marriages.

But it is hard to break old habits. So a Church that has new permission for more understanding, humanity, creativity, and caring still has a tendency to function legalistically. In Europe and America the annulment process is almost the only known way for the Catholic to remarry. The Church is making the process more accessible to a wider range of people, but it is doing so by increasing the personnel and efficiency of its marriage courts and expanding its reasons for legitimate annulments. It is a step forward although, unfortunately, a legalistic one.

Like a good steward, the Church could bring out of its richness of tradition simple forgiveness for failure, the concept of death other than physical in a marriage, the awareness of when there is sacrilege rather than sacrament, and the power to understand that when little has been given, little is required. The same steward might point out the fact that of the 102 conferences of bishops the world over, sixty-five percent do not even have marriage tribunals. They simply deal effectively and responsibly according to the needs of their culture to keep Christ vibrant and alive in their communities after a marriage failure.

Catholics today stand at a critical time in marital history in which there is both opportunity and danger. The Church is questioning itself after centuries of fighting for the ideal in marriage in the midst of conflict and opposition. It teeters between falling back into the protective armor and deceptive safety of legalism or venturing into creative theologies about the strength and weakness of humanity, its failure and redemption, its agony and its ecstasy.

# 4. Viewpoints: The Varying Positions on Divorce and Remarriage Within the Church

Considering the various ways the Scripture passages on divorce and remarriage can be read and the variety of applications down through history, it might not come as a surprise to discover that there are different Church viewpoints today on the subject. A discerning mind might find these varying viewpoints exciting, while the mind comfortable only with uniformity will find them exasperating.

The Roman Catholic position on divorce and remarriage can be said to fall into three categories. Jesus' clear prohibition of divorce and remarriage can be taken: as an absolute, without exception, for all marriages; divorce and remarriage as are wrong (illicit) but forgivable; or as an ideal to be attempted in marriage. The present popular theoretical position of the Church is the first, that is, that sacramental marriages are final and without exception. Again, as in history, the Church's practice is more merciful than its theory. The longest tradition of the Church is the second, that remarriage is illicit but forgivable. The third position, of one marriage as the ideal, has been mentioned in the Western tradition of the Church with little support, although it has effectively been used in the Eastern tradition.

## INDISSOLUBLE WITHOUT EXCEPTION

It must be said that those who espouse the first position tend to be severe, legal, and absolute. Without question, Jesus' teaching takes a definite stand against divorce and remarriage, but to the legalist this applies to all marriages without exception as a moral imperative. It is also the present theoretical position of the Catholic Church.

In favor of this position are the following points:
Jesus' position was certainly for the permanency of marriage. Society is certainly stronger when there is permanency in marriage. The very nature of the marriage vows explicitly intends permanency. Children have a greater sense of security. The permanency of marriage evokes a greater sense of commitment and responsibility in all human contracts and promises.

Not in favor of this position are the following points:
Jesus designates only one unforgivable sin and that is against the Holy Spirit, not the one of divorce and remarriage.

Jesus acknowledges varying abilities; from those who have been given much, much is required . . . some are given ten talents, some five, and some one. Jesus does not use the word "indissoluble" or the phrase ". . . man *cannot*"; Jesus uses the phrase ". . . *let not* man.*"

"What God has put joined . . ." That is exactly the question; there may be marriages that God did not put together.

"Until death do us part." Why do those in Western culture take this to mean there is only one death, that of the body? There are other forms of death.

In some cases, enforced permanency endangers the individuals in a marriage.

Three of the five basic Scripture passages of the New Testament have exception clauses. If Matthew and Paul understood Jesus as declaring marriage an indissoluble bond, they would hardly have felt free to introduce modifications. It seems clear that Matthew and Paul understood Jesus to be declaring a general principle or guiding rule.

Many of the renowned Christian writers up to the fourteenth century did not interpret Jesus' comments on divorce and remarriage as absolute. Some of these were Tertullian, Origen of Alexandria, Lactantius, Saint Basil the Great, Pope Gregory II, and several other popes. Pope Alexander III, the first canon lawyer to become pope, considered remarriage illicit but not invalid.

## WRONG (ILLICIT) BUT FORGIVABLE

This concept does not have the stifling absolutism of the first position on indissolubility or the ethereal disposition of the third in which Jesus' words are taken as an ideal. In favor of this position are all the objections listed against those who hold indissolubility as a moral imperative. The list is quite impressive because it does embrace the exception clauses of Scripture and the position certainly is affirmed in tradition, even in papal pronouncements.

A consideration not in its favor focuses on a weakness of human nature, that of people making excuses for themselves. Or, to use the rather unfortunate term of our century, people might have the tendency to "rationalize" a divorce from a spouse for any difficulty encountered. This line of thought is principally founded in the fear that the weakness of human nature will achieve supremacy over its virtue.

## THE IDEAL

Those who have a high regard for human nature and appeal to its noble qualities generally gravitate toward Scripture as an ideal. Such people are repelled by the school of thought that looks upon Scripture as a moral imperative. Their plea is that you have to be free to love. They rely heavily on trust in human nature and the mercy of God.

The weakness of this position lies in the difficulty of trying to organize groups of people without directives. Utopian ideals appear attractive but are hard to implement when people angrily scream for direction. The Church has usually found itself in the position of dealing with nations of people demanding direction.

## TOLERATING REMARRIAGE

While philosophers and theorists speculate, people work out their practice in the streets. Sometimes people are influenced by pronouncements from above, sometimes not. The theories that permit divorce and remarriage are four. The first three have the force of long historical tradition and the fourth is a bonafide position of many Church moral theologians today. These theories are the sin theory, the death theory, the annulment theory, and the preference principle theory.

## THE SIN THEORY

Historically the Church dealt with divorce as it did with any other sin or failure. If it were personal sin that terminated the marriage, the one who sinned was led to repentance. If the marriage was a human mistake and neither sinned, this "objective" sin against the permancy of marriage was forgiven. After this the two people were free to enter a second marriage. Admittedly this was not the ideal since it was a second marriage. Nevertheless it was considered blessed by God and sacred. In the early centuries the Church accepted the state's control over the practice of marriage, divorce, and remarriage. By so doing, the Church ratified the Roman Empire's position against divorce but, like the government, still allowed it when the marriage failed. The Christian community certainly did not go along with the empire's position with regard to war, murder in the circuses, lewd plays, and prostitution. Eventually devout Christian leaders in the Empire accepted the reality of divorce and addressed it with understanding. The experience of the leaders was that adultery, violence, abandonment, and many forms of abuse were not to be tolerated in marriage. Such marriages could be, and in some cases should be, terminated. In the minds of the civil leaders it would be an injustice to demand that the innocent party be punished with no opportunity of remarriage because of the failure of his or her spouse.

In the beginning of Christianity the state controlled marriages, so the Church did not reflect deeply on the nature of the problem of remarriage. Simple forgiveness was the Church's response to a marriage failure and remarriage was allowed.

The simplicity of the Church practice flowed naturally from its concept of marriage. Marriage was looked upon as a relationship. If the relationship failed, even through sin, it could be forgiven if there was repentance, thus allowing a second marriage. In later centuries the marriage relationship was considered more in its sexual than in its spiritual nature. This particularly surfaces in the theory that the consummation of marriage takes place at the first act of intercourse after the wedding. Naturally in a second marriage there would be intercourse and according to this theory each act of intercourse in the second relationship would be adulterous to the first. However, if the parties of the second marriage lived as brother and sister, they could remain together without sin. If marriage is seen primarily as sexual union, such a conclusion is logical. If marriage is seen primarily as a relationship, such a solution is preposterous. It was only after the first millennium and the entrance of legalistic thought into theology that marriage was looked on more for its sexual activity than its spiritual relationship and the simple solution for remarriage of the first thousand years was minimized. However, it can be ironically observed that this sexual approach to marriage was contrived by celibate theologians.

Remarriage as the unforgivable sin widened the breach with the Protestants after the Reformation and was an ongoing source of loss of membership from the Catholic Church. This is to say nothing of the agonizing damage that it did to conscientious Catholics who knew they could not live without marital companionship after marriage failure. Disbelief was heightened when these individuals knew what a tragedy the first marriage had been.

It might be said that the simple solution for remarriage in the earlier Church is implicitly in Scripture in the concept of forgiveness. However, neither the Catholic nor the Protestant position is explicitly in Scripture. Both positions are tenable. The position an individual or group assumes will be largely determined by cultural practices and personal persuasion.

## THE DEATH THEORY

It is very difficult to trace the date when the death theory reached complete form. Somewhere in the sixth or seventh century is a legitimate guess. It evolved out of a concept of marriage as a relationship and is more evident in Eastern cultures even today than in those of the West.

This theory looks at the words of the marriage vow "until death do us part." In the Eastern/Oriental view a person is more than just a body, and beside physical death there also occur moral, psychological, and political death. These concepts of the different kinds of death are still held among some Roman Catholics in the Eastern rite and by the Orthodox.

The people of this culture recognize different kinds of marriage. A convenantal marriage is one that reflects the permanent commitment of Christ to his Church. A person entering a covenantal marriage would not remarry even in the event of the death of a spouse. A covenantal marriage occurs only once in a lifetime. But a marriage that was entered into after the physical death of a spouse can be a sacred marriage or even a sacramental one. But in the eastern culture death can be physical, moral, psychological, or spiritual. Such a second marriage could be holy and pleasing to God. If a person entered a third or later marriage, he or she could do so honorably, but the appraisal of such a marriage would be left to the discretion of God.

## Physical Death

Physical death in the East and the West is the same; it is the stopping of the human heart and the decay of the body.

## Moral Death

Moral death takes place when the affection of one of the parties of marriage is either destroyed or ceases of its own accord after some period of time. People who experience moral death often refer to it as "nothing left," "the relationship is dead," or "something died inside." Certain human actions can destroy affection. Such actions as incest, murder, violence, or betrayal can cause love to be changed into repulsion. Disappearance, long absences in the relationship, one's inability for psychological intimacy, and alcoholism sometimes cause affection and love to dwindle and die.

At the exhilarating National Conference of the Divorced and Separated at Notre Dame University, a priest gave an outstanding talk on the concept of annulment. After his lucid presentation one of the women came up to him and asked him what she should do if she wanted to remarry and felt that her first marriage was valid. The speaker invited her to go for a walk where they could quietly discuss her concerns. In sight of the golden dome of the university, they walked along the pathway of the neatly cut lawns of the university grounds. She told her story.

"Father, my husband and I were deeply in love at the time of our marriage. We were both from good Catholic families, and we both had earned our masters degrees at Catholic universities. I certainly cannot say we were not prepared to marry at twenty-four years of age; we were both holding down competent jobs and trying to live our faith in the secular world. We began our family and eventually moved to a different part of the country as my husband excelled in his work.

"I can remember distinctly. It was after our tenth anniversary.

He began drinking and often failed to come home for supper in the evenings. His departure from our lifestyle was dramatically revealed to me one day when I came home unexpectedly and found him in bed with someone else. Like a naughty boy who lashes out, he began to hit me. I was very stern and told him I would not tolerate that.

"Three months later he came home about one o'clock in the morning. I got up when he entered our bedroom, put on my bathrobe, and confronted him with his behavior. With a powerful open hand he slapped me on the side of the head and almost knocked me out. I looked up at him from the floor and heard him say, 'You bitch, get out of my life!'

"I remember distinctly saying within my heart, 'You son-of-a-bitch, you *are* out of my life!' Something died inside of me then. I don't know why, but I knew I would never be able to live with that man again. Something died inside of me. Your talk was brilliant, Father, but it doesn't apply to me. We had a valid marriage, but it *died* ten years later. I do not want to remain single, but I will never go back to him. What do I do?"

Without a doubt a great amount of discernment and caution has to be exercised in detecting whether there is actual moral death in a troubled marriage or merely exhaustion, temporary loss of hope, or severe anger. Often separation, counseling, or a human tragedy can revive a critically ill relationship. The marital relationship might never return to its original condition, but it could well be functional and be enriched with other aspects of loyalty, heroism, or undaunted love. However, if hatred or repulsion remains after a period of time, an analysis of the relationship might show it to be dead more than dying.

### Psychological Death

The most obvious forms of psychological death are mind or brain disorders for which there is no cure. A clear example of this is the "human vegetable" whose mind does not function because of an inoperable tumor causing insanity, severe physical brain damage, or lack of oxygen to the brain.

It was June 15, 1973, when Dan and Alyce had a colorful and joyful marriage in a common chapel in Kansas City. Alyce's cousin was a priest who was in residence there while he was pursuing some specialized studies. Both Dan and Alyce were devout Catholics and, at the ages of twenty-eight and twenty-seven, looked forward to a loving and exciting life together. Not only that, their families had known each other and had interacted on social, religious, and educational levels. The reception lasted late into the evening with parents, brothers, sisters, and friends having a raucously good time.

The next morning some of the family saw Dan and Alyce off on their honeymoon to the Virgin Islands. They arrived safely and went to the hotel. They swam, had a candlelight supper, and retired for the night. The next morning, in their new sport clothes, they rented some motorbikes to tour the island. Then tragedy struck.

Dan was coming down a hill at a rather high speed when a water tanker pulled out from a wooded area. Dan tried to stop but could not. He crouched over and tried to go under the tanker. In an instant he was unseated as his head and shoulders smashed against the side of the water tank and his bike continued to race forward. At the sound of the impact, the driver halted the rig and jumped out. Both Alyce and the driver rushed to Dan's side. Blood was coming from his mouth, nose, and ears. For days Dan was comatose and Alyce kept vigil in the hospital. The diagnosis was unanimous: if Dan ever recovered consciousness, he would be mentally incompetent.

A few weeks later Dan was flown back to Kansas City and placed in extended care. Seven years passed, and Dan still remained alive. Alyce's visits became less frequent within a couple of years.

As must be, she had to make new decisions about the direction her life would take. Seven years later, she visited her cousin priest, asking to be married again. Brian was the potential groom's name —a Catholic, never married before, a successful attorney, and a gentle and caring man.

Father Jim shook his head at the request for marriage saying, "Alyce, you can never get an annulment for your marriage. You said the marriage was consummated, and there would be no way to establish at this time any deficiencies in the contract. An annulment is out of the question."

Alyce did not see the logic. "But Jim," she protested, "how can a Church that reverances life and encourages the begetting of children deprive a person like me of having children when I want them so badly? Dan is dead! You heard what the doctor said. Why can't the Church accept that?"

Father Jim stared down for a moment, shook his head in obvious regret, looked up at his cousin and said, "Alyce, I can't help you. All I can say is, follow your conscience."

Alyce went on to press her case. "Jim, I don't like that answer. Maybe it's the way the Church taught me, but when I am following my own conscience I feel like I'm doing something sneaky, making up my own rules, rationalizing. If following my own conscience is really the teaching of the Church, why can't *it* act on it and provide some form of ceremony for what is truly lawful?"

Again, in the Eastern Catholic tradition, such a misfortune would not create a problem for a second marriage. Brain deterioration for which there is no expected improvement, such as occurs in senility, Alzheimer's disease, or damage by drugs, are other recognized forms of psychological death. Harder to recognize are character disorders, actual changes of personality that seem permanent, that occur after marriage. The theorist or hurting spouse is left in a quandary as to whether or not the death theory could actually be used in justifying remarriage.

The associate pastor at Saint Mary's Church in Phoenix, Arizona, was also chaplain of the Arizona State Hospital within the city's confines. One day when he was visiting the ward, he happened to meet a woman who was listed as a Roman Catholic. Her hair was disheveled, her eyes were blank and her jaw dropped; she was totally out of contact with reality. Her name, however, was familiar. She had the same last name of one of the most prominent men in the parish. He was married and had four children who were in the parochial school. He was on the school board and very active in raising funds for Catholic education. The priests of the parish called upon him repeatedly in times of need. He was an exemplary Catholic.

The curiosity of the hospital chaplain mounted as the days went on. One day at a parish bazaar, the priest entered into a conversation with the man. He was very candid with him, saying, "John, I'm not going to blow the whistle, but I'm terribly curious. I've come across Mary Lebaki at the state hospital. I've inquired about her, and they told me that she was your first wife. Is that true?"

Without hesitation, John answered, "Yes."

The priest shook his head in puzzlement and said, "John, I can't imagine you being married outside the Church. Were you married in the Church to Mary?"

The man answered, "Yes."

"Were you married in the Church to Diane? How can you be going to Communion?" asked the priest.

John laughed and answered, "Father, I was married the second time right here at Saint Mary's Church. I am Lebanese. I am of the Byzantine rite. Mary entered the state hospital only three months after our wedding. No one had the slightest idea why she became ill. Doctors have given the illness many names, but the reality is that she appeared to be perfectly normal until she became mentally ill. I visited her in the state hospital almost daily for a year. The visits became less frequent during the next two years. I was told that she would never recover. Eight years later I fell in love with Diane. When this occurred, I called the regional bishop. He actually came to Phoenix and talked to the psychiatrist. When he found out that there was no recovery from Mary's mental illness, he proclaimed the death of that marriage and performed the wedding of Diane and me at Saint Mary's Church, right here in Phoenix, Arizona."

*Political Death*

Political death takes place when a person is taken into slavery, sentenced to life imprisonment, or chooses a political career that takes that individual permanently from the marriage. It might be noted that this theory was used in the United States during the time of slavery for black slaves. Many of the slaves of Irish and French masters wanted to convert to the Catholic religion of their lords. Since most of them had been married in Africa but did not know where their spouses were, Rome gave them permission to be baptized and remarried or retain a second marriage already made here based on the political death theory.

THE ANNULMENT THEORY

The Evangelists Matthew and Mark use the words "Let no man separate what God has joined." As mentioned before, when the Christian community tackled with the issue of divorce and remarriage in the twelfth century, it began to ask the question "Has God put this marriage together?" Because the annulment theory developed at a time of legalism in the Church, a simple analysis of it is difficult. It is fraught with theoretical possibilities and an endless list of human variables. The simplicity of the sin and death theories is utterly absent in the theory of annulment. This theory is virtually used only in Europe and America today.

The theories of sin, death, and the preference principle (developed later) appreciate a marriage existentially, that is, as it is now, its current condition. Unlike these, the annulment theory has only to do with the time the marriage was performed. Both parties of the relationship seeking annulment are appraised according to a checklist for their capability of entering a Christian marriage at the very time of the wedding.

Clearly stated, then, the annulment process has to do with a Church tradition, not a civil one. This distinction is critically important because many Roman Catholics are appalled to think that they are asked to deny the existence of a marriage that was acknowledged and witnessed by family and friends, had binding implications and ramifications civilly, and from which children may have been born. For these people, acknowledging that that marriage never existed is repulsive and a lie. However, if the same individuals were asked if the relationship was sacred or if they really thought God had put that marriage together, the response is often an emphatic no. Was there a marriage? "Yes." Was there a Christian marriage? "No."

Some grounds for annulment are easy to determine—one or both participants weren't old enough, there was too close of a blood relationship, an unknown previous marriage, or a real intention not to be faithful, or the marriage was not performed by a proper authority. When there is a problem determining grounds for annulment, we have to make decisions in human matters that only God can know the truth of. Did the person lack psychological age (maturity) when he or she showed responsibility in other matters? How much fear constitutes enough to nullify a marriage? Was there enough cultural or family pressure to constitute force? In a marriage that eventually fails, how can we be certain whether the capability was there in the beginning or if it dissolved as time went on? Was the inability to establish a permanent relationship in seed from the beginning or not? We are truly making decisions on earth that God alone knows in heaven. For some people the annulment process clarifies the reality. For other people it veils it even more. For the first there is comfort; for the second there is agony or a feeling of futility.

## Advantages

The annulment process is very appealing to the legal, Western mind, for it is only in Western culture that we receive a printed-out receipt for a tube of toothpaste or a five-ounce apple from the supermarket. To validate our human accomplishments, we need a receipt. An annulment satisfies that kind of mind.

In a small town in central California, two participants in a divorced support group approached the priest chaplain for an annulment. During the interview, the priest learned that both parties of the marriage knew that they were not the marrying kind of people. The marriage was a standoff between two people who wanted to be single. When the priest inquired if either ever intended to marry again, there was an emphatic "never." Puzzled, the priest asked why they wanted an annulment if they never intended to marry again. "Oh, Father, we would not feel part of the Church unless we went through an annulment."

Annulment is an affirmation by the Catholic religious tradition that a person of faith has made a human mistake. The proclamation that a marriage was not intended by God is extremely comforting for many faithful individuals. When the process reveals deception, immaturity, or the incapability of entering a marriage of religious quality, it is of great comfort to some people. The annulment process also puts an official end to a relationship that may have been a nightmare.

In Atlanta a middle-aged man of about forty-five came to the parish rectory in search of a priest who would assist him in the annulment process. The priest asked if he would be so kind as to review the marriage history to see if an annulment were appropriate. The visitor began with the time twenty years before when he had married a beautiful girl, expecting a life marriage of happiness and love.

"Six months after the marriage she became exceedingly sloppy. Though she was pregnant by then, she began staying out at night.

The baby was born, and I came home to my beautiful wife who was drunk or stoned, or else she was out with someone else with the baby. Eventually there were more babies—who were left by open windows in winter, wandering out in the street, you name it, it happened. There were four pregnancies, and I'm not sure all of the kids are mine; $55,000 worth of bills from doctors and institutions; two terribly disturbed kids; and lawsuits by neighbors. I was never going to get divorced because my Church is against it, my family is against it, and I'm against it. Then my son committed suicide, leaving a note saying that he wanted to go someplace where there was happiness. I finally accepted the reality that I was in a sacrilege, not a sacrament. I don't care what it costs, I need to be cleansed of that evil."

The process of sitting down and responding to questions about a marriage can be healing in itself, for some. This process can lead them to forgiveness of themselves or of the other spouse. It can make people confront the problem and accept their responsibility in the marriage failure or help them recognize any negative behavior they may have assumed just for survival.

The annulment process can not only be permission for another marriage, but also quality preparation for it by making one aware of what is needed for a good marital relationship. On a larger scale, the theory of annulment allows greater recognition of the qualities of a true marriage required by Jesus than the other theories.

## Disadvantages

The annulment process is for the sophisticated and the educated. It demands a gathering of documents, the ability to read and write, and almost a college education to properly decipher the shades of meaning in the legal terminology. People from the Third World and minority groups have trouble thinking in these terms and responding to them. Over sixty percent of the Roman Catholic Church episcopates throughout the world do not have tribunals for this process and a lesser percentage have ineffective ones. So the annulment process is highly discriminatory toward some of God's people.

Although the annulment process was recognized in the twelfth century, its popularity did not dawn until just a few decades ago. Before the Code of 1917, the process was so cumbersome that a person had to be among the royality even to afford the number of lawyers necessary for the process. Even as late as 1968 there were only 338 annulments granted. The numbers swelled to 52,000 by 1983, a 15,000 percent increase in just fifteen years. At the same time it must be remembered that the divorce increase did not escalate to epidemic proportions until after the Second World War.

Some individuals have been so psychologically damaged in hellish marriages that they have had to have extensive counseling in order to lead productive lives again. The detailed recounting necessary for the annulment process might dangerously tip the scales toward pathology again. In other cases an irascible individual might be so angered by a Church process or "just another process" that custody proceedings might be renewed, child support withdrawn, inheritance altered, or a family feud fanned to explosion.

The annulment process cannot be justly used for those marriages that were truly valid Christian marriages at their inception. The annulment procedure acknowledges only one termination of a truly valid marriage, and that is physical death. Though this tradition has only been effective in the Church for less than seven hundred years and is derived from a culture far more sophisticated than that in which Jesus lived, it is still the only predominently acknowledged process of dealing with Catholic marriage failure in the English-speaking world and is the only process in some sectors.

Heather and Jack were both full-time students at the University of California at Berkeley. Jack was a brilliant individual who was studying law. Heather was equally brilliant and pursuing her studies in English. Both attended the campus Newman Center and participated in all of its activities. They were described as an unusually devout pair. It was part of this common devotion that led them to eventually become engaged to each other and a year later to be married at the Paulist Newman Center near the campus. Jack had another year to finish school after the marriage. Heather was willing to help support him through this last year. Jack graduated and passed his bar exam without difficulty.

The couple moved to a small town in the Mother Lode country of California where they settled down and became part of the parish community. Three children were born of the marriage. Their extended family and friends thought them the ideal couple and family.

Seven years after the marriage, an attractive, free-wheeling secretary came to work at the flourishing law practice that Jack had established. Looking back, Heather could remember "that woman" having some type of a power over Jack. The story was typical. He began by being late for supper and then missing supper. Soon he had extended meetings that kept him to 10:30, 11:00, and 11:30 at night. All of a sudden he had business trips that took him out of town, something that was unusual for his practice. When Heather objected to many of these antics, Jack became angry. As if in defiance, he was seen in public and at parties and socials with his secretary. Finally Jack moved in with his secretary and filed for divorce.

The devastation was overwhelming for Heather. She could not face her parish community or the townspeople. After an agonizing four months of hoping against hope that Jack would come to his senses, she finally moved out of town. Jack's personality had truly changed. When the divorce was final, Heather knew in her heart he would never return.

Heather became part of the parish activity and leadership in her new location. The priest, seeing the grace with which she participated in people's lives and the care she showered upon her children, began speaking with her about an annulment just in case remarriage occurred for her in the future.

Heather insisted that there was no possibility. She had read many books about the concept of annulment and its process. She insisted that she and Jack had a valid marriage. There was no sign prior to the marriage that would predict his change of personality, no hint of similar disintegration of ideals and religious dedication in any of Jack's family members.

Father Joe insisted that the canon lawyers might be able to find something that she did not recognize. Heather graciously admitted that that was always a possibility, but she had done reading and research looking for that something herself. They had both certainly been responsible people prior to the marriage. They had seven years of a very happy and healthy relationship. There was no indication of mental illness that could be traced to the family or prior to the wedding. Heather was firm and maintained that no amount of casuistry of the law, expertise of lawyers, or loophole finding could ever allow her to be comfortable with a Church decision for an annulment of her marriage.

A large number of marriages that have ended in divorce cannot be proven as invalid. The annulment process is a legal process and needs evidence and witnesses. Sometimes the reason for the marriage failure is known to the person alone and, legally, nobody can judge his or her own case.

In 1984, in the Midwest, a man approached one of the priests who often assisted with Beginning Experience, a nationwide program for the divorced sponsored by the Catholic Church. The man told the priest that he had spent forty-two years in a hellish marriage. When he finally broke from his wife, she promised to sue him for everything he had.

"That typified our entire married life," he said. "I finally had enough courage to leave that marriage four years ago. Now I have met a wonderful Catholic woman who is a widow. She obviously wants to marry in the Catholic Church, as do I, so I need an annulment from my previous marriage." The man went on to add that for many years he had taught in a parochial school, and he felt that he would not be allowed to continue if he married outside the Church.

In a very forthright way the priest asked him, "Why do you think your marriage was invalid?"

The man replied, "Father, I never wanted to marry her. This is a true story. She was from a very strong Catholic Italian family. I'm not Italian—I'm one of those Heinz-57 varieties. You won't believe this, but this is the truth. The second time I dated my wife, I went over to her house and was surrounded by five very large brothers. They looked me over and approved. Believe me, from that time on, the family planned the wedding. I didn't have enough guts to stop the whole process. The mother actually told me when I should give her the engagement ring. Like a stupid idiot, I followed all of this as though I had better not change my mind.

"It was decided that two of the brothers would be my best men. At the wedding rehearsals I knew that the whole thing was all wrong. I did not love this woman and I did not want to marry her. What was I doing here? After the wedding practice I excused myself, went out to the car and a very strong voice within me said, 'You are absolutely dishonest. What are you doing marrying this woman? Get into that car and run for your life.' Actually two of the brothers came out and got me before I could get into the car.

"You won't believe this, Father, but I almost fainted on my wedding day, because I knew it was wrong. Her family kidded about it as they gave me smelling salts. She dominated my life, and the family dominated her life.

"Father, we had a biological marriage. When she wanted a child, we had intercourse. When she did not, we did not have intercourse. The first major decision I have ever made in my life was when I divorced her to start a life of my own."

The priest inquired whether he had ever put his opposition to the marriage in writing or whether he had ever told anyone—a brother, best friend, or anyone. The answer was, "Father, I was too scared and too shy to do anything like that. Except for the fact that I almost fainted, there was no indication of my mortal fear and repulsion for this marriage except within me."

The priest pressed him to try to recall if he had told anybody of his fear and of his repulsion to marry this person. "I told no one," he answered.

"To all exterior appearances, that marriage was successful," the priest remarked. "I do not know what to do, because no one can be a judge in his own case. You have all of the reasons for an annulment, but absolutely no proof. You will have to make some conscience decisions for yourself."

Immediately the gray-haired man replied, "I have finally found courage within me to make such a decision. My only problem is that I am sixty years old and cannot enter the public school system after all these years of teaching in a parochial school. If I marry outside the Church, I know I will lose my job. Furthermore, I know the one I want to marry, and she wants to marry me. However, she feels that she would never be married unless it was within the Church. I can follow my conscience, but I don't think the parochial school system would accept that. Neither would my intended."

There are times when witnesses are lacking. At other times the glib articulation of one party overwhelms the clumsy presentation of the other. And there are times when proceeding with the annulment process would actually be a danger for some innocent party.

In the archdiocese of Los Angeles, Father Walter was teaching a course on marriage at a Catholic college. He emphatically proclaimed that the Church should stand firm in its opposition to second marriages, especially in this era of collapsing contracts. He maintained that the Church should keep the penalty of prohibiting parties of second marriages who have not secured ecclesiastical approval through annulment from participating in the sacraments.

A priest friend in a nearby parish, Father Charles, maintained that such punishment was cruel. Jesus came for the sick and the poor, and forbidding Communion hindered their access to him. Father Charles took remarrying couples through a process of discussion over options (among which was a possible pastoral solution), prayer, discernment, and decision. With equal enthusiasm, Father Charles insisted that his position was the one the Church should take.

A few months later, Ronald, a military companion of Father Walter, came to him for help with his fiancée, Jean Louise. She had been married previously, but the marriage had been a disaster from the start. Her former husband had been a very stoic, cold, calculating person. He was a living computer, even in his lovemaking. It was painful for Jean Louise to recall that marriage. It was a nightmare!

After the marriage finally terminated in divorce, her former husband approached her one day when she was getting into the car, looked her straight in the eye, and said with a penetrating, steel-cold look, "I will dismember you if I ever hear from you again." After a five-second vicious stare that terrified her, he walked away.

Ronald, a doctor, had a personality check done on that man. What his fiancée maintained was quite true. Even her former spouse's colleagues were not comfortable with him. As a few members of this man's staff reported, "He's strange."

Without hesitation, Ronald said to Father Walter, pointing to Jean Louise, "She is not going through an annulment. Someone may end up dead!"

Father Walter listened to his friend sympathetically and recommended a priest friend of his who worked in one of the nearby parishes. "He is very good with these impossible situations," Father Walter said.

After consultation with Father Charles, a pastoral solution was obviously selected. The wedding arrangements were made, and both priests concelebrated with Father Charles hearing the vows because Father Walter was not comfortable with that. The wedding ceremony was beautiful. The Eucharist was shared by all.

In the sacristy, fully vested in priestly garments, Charles kicked Walter in the backside and lively jested, "You fire and brimstone prophet! What did you proclaim on *that* one? It finally hit home, didn't it?"

Perhaps part of the human experience is to acknowledge with humility that we can usually be certain about objective truth until it becomes personal.

Regardless of the oath taken to tell the truth, angry or vengeful people may lie during annulment proceedings. By the same token, if evidence is taken from a schizophrenic spouse or witness, it remains a schizophrenic testimony.

When a person proclaims that he or she has gotten a "Church annulment" it sounds as though God has spoken. Yet this procedure is laced with so many human elements that error unfortunately seems inevitable.

The word "Church" has an awesome sound to it. This is how it should be, since Jesus promised to be with it until the end of time. However, once a person begins to walk the corridors of the institution and meet its people, it becomes less awesome. Without irreverence, one must often challenge the dispensers of God's mercy in that Church. After a thorough study of tribunal procedure, Theodore Davey wrote:

Thus it is asserted that if one judges marriage tribunals by their effectiveness in upholding the sacredness and meaning of Christian marriage and by their provision of justice for the Catholic faithful, then they fail on both accounts.[23]

Church courts, tribunals, have personalities. Some are known to process annulments quickly and with great latitude; others are known to be slow, and severe. If the annulment process of the Catholic Church were the only means of dispensing God's mercy and freedom, there would be fear about "localized salvation."

On one occasion a divorced and remarried person visited a

priest in Billings, Montana, requesting an annulment for the previous marriage so that she could go back to the sacraments. However, her present husband had just secured a job in a Midwestern diocese. As frequently occurs, the priest was not only the pastor of the parish, but also an advocate on the tribunal.

In the presence of the petitioner, the priest phoned a knowledgable judge of the diocesan tribunal whom he knew. He was put through to his judge friend. "I have a woman who is going to be moving in one month. She is very anxious about getting the procedure taken care of in order to get back to the sacraments. My first response is to have her begin the annulment process in the diocese to which she is going, but I wanted to check with you first. What is your reaction to that?"

Fortunately, the priest had the ear part of the phone pressed closely against his ear. "For the love of God, Ben, have her maintain some kind of a residence here among her friends or relatives, and we will process it here. The bishop where she is going is an old canon law professor. He will not allow his tribunal members to process any cases without his complete surveilance. He has processed five annulments in six years."

Without registering any surprise, the priest acknowledged the response. "Doug, you're a good man. See you next Thursday." He then reached into his file cabinet for the proper forms while he commented to his inquirer, "It is best that we begin the procedure here."

Obviously, if salvation depended upon a human process, redemption would be localized.

A tribunal is not an "it," but a group of people whose competency ranges with the same variations as in any other institution. Many tribunals leave testimony taking to local priests who may be very holy men but incompetent legally. And the awesome position of judge requires a great deal. In the national journal for canon lawyers, *The Jurist,* the position of judge (often a priest of the diocese without canonical training) is described as follows:

The expertise of the judge will be defined according to the issue he is called upon to decide and according to the type of evidence presented. The judge is always an expert in the law of marriage and procedures. It would seem the judge is also an expert in rational psychology and moral theology. With a background of philosophy and theology, with an understanding of the principles of decision-making in morality, a knowledge of the moral-personal aspects of the celebration of a sacrament, the judge would have quite impressive competence to evaluate evidence given concerning the human act of consent for marriage.[24]

## Process Immoral

At the Southwest Regional Canon Law Conference held at the Franciscan Renewal Center in Scottsdale, Arizona, the merits and liabilities of the annulment process were being discussed by the various tribunal members. A priest from the tribunal of Tucson stood up in the middle of his forty colleagues and said he thought the entire annulment process was immoral. Rippling across his audience were expressions of stark wonder, anger, surprise, humor, and indifference. The chairman asked the one making the comment to elaborate. Without hesitation he stated that the system was contrary to the gospel message.

Jesus maintained clearly to the Pharisees that the law was made for people and not people for the law, and many civil governments such as that of the United States presume a person innocent until proven guilty. Not so with canon law. The assumption of canon law is that where there is a doubt, one is to favor the law and not the people.

The priest from Tucson had been in tribunal work for many years, and not once had he ever heard tribunal members encourage a person to follow his or her own conscience when the annulment decision was negative, even when the lawyers on the case did not know whether to grant it or not. He continued that in his diocese Indians, Hispanics, blacks, and Caucasians were all treated the same way in a process that favors Caucasians. Chicanos were asked to produce baptismal certificates when many of them did not even know how to write or were aware of any certificates ever being recorded. He lamented the fact that during the past year seven directives had gone out to priests about different tribunal procedural processes and not one had encouraged priests to use the pastoral solution. Heads began to nod in agreement among the canon lawyers, but he was not finished.

"As all of you know, according to law, a priest should never refuse a person who presents himself or herself for Communion.

Why haven't more of those people been encouraged to present themselves who feel in their hearts that God approves of a second marriage though the Church is unable to deal with it?" Turning to the entire group he asked, "Which one of you has ever done that —has ever used that section of the mercy of law?" There was a stillness. Eyebrows rose in amazement and in recognition.

"There are many secretarial desks in our tribunals to judge marriage failures. Where is the altar to bless the new marriage? Jesus sat down by the well and talked to the woman divorced five times about the Kingdom of God and about salvation. Which one of us has ever done that? We sit down with the one who has been married only once before and threaten him or her with loss of salvation if they marry again and even add some thoughtless remark about excommunication. We act like we are God, but we don't act *like* God. Our very office itself is entitled 'tribunal,' like we are a medieval court that puts thumbs up or thumbs down on people's lives and destinies. Why don't we at least call it a 'Council of Discernment for God's Love'?"

There was stillness over the conference room. As the speaker paused and looked down, it was difficult to detect whether his expression reflected sorrow or shame. As though the chairman was wondering himself, he asked the speaker in a very gentle, searching way, "John, with those feelings, why are you even a part of the tribunal?"

The instant response was, "To make the system of the Church less immoral."

Then, turning to the audience again with surprising confidence, he continued, "Gentlemen," and on second glance added, "and lovely ladies," almost parenthetically lowering his voice to address the men. "If we would have added these ladies years ago, maybe there would be less brutality and more mercy in what we are doing. They have added gentleness and intuition." Raising his voice with a touch of defiance, "I have remained a part of the tribunal to make it less immoral. I have a tribunal within a tribunal. I have a desk of legalism for our educated who find it inconsequential to pay for long distance calls to summon a certificate and who officiously pronounce, 'I will type this and it will be on your desk tomorrow morning.' I give them the satisfaction of knowing that we are as businesslike as they and equally as efficient. I Xerox a notarized copy and return it to them. I can just hear them say, 'Ah, the Church is so modern.'

"But I also have a desk for the simple, the confused, and the uneducated. I listen to their story and, as though they are the teachers, ask them to help me understand. Then in veiled ways I ask them technical questions about certificates and witnesses. More often than not they shake their heads, knit their brows, and their silence says very loudly, 'I don't understand. I have told you everything I know.'

"So I put on my vestments and take them to my altar. We say some prayers, and I bless them and pronounce them beautiful before God. We hug, laugh a little, and they walk away saying something like, 'How merciful God is.'"

Unexpectedly the speaker concluded by sitting down. Lost in thought, the assembly sat in silence as though knowing that anything after that would have no value. The priest chairman said, "I think it's time for a break."

The new code of canon law (November 27, 1983) has brought in new considerations for the person applying for an annulment. For one thing, four to eight weeks may be added for the length of the process. The old code could be said to be very humane. In it the Church tried to veer away from adversary terms like "defendant" and "plaintiff." Annulment was not a process to find out who the "bad" person was and spouses never had to face each other because it was a "paper process." The cost was usually far less than any civil annulment or divorce and could be waived in the case of poverty. However, the new code has an added procedure called "publication of the acts." Spouses may read each other's testimony. This may well cut down on the freedom of response or catapult the whole process into the conflict of adversaries.

And it is estimated that it will cost another $2 million a year to operate the whole tribunal system in the United States because a single judge can no longer decide cases. This does not seem to be a vote of confidence for the tribunal system at least in America. People who are conscious of social justice issues find it hard to understand why the institution would make the annulment process more onerous, taking more money and ministerial time when both of these could be used for more life-giving causes.

Many priests feel so overburdened in the needs of the ministry now that they don't like to cooperate with the complicated annulment procedure. The estimate of the number of Roman Catholics who are in a second marriage or are contemplating a second marriage or are planning a marriage with a divorced person is nearing nine million. Seven years ago, of all those who appealed to the Church for help, only five percent would even be heard. If that were even doubled for our time, it would still be like trying to take care of an epidemic with Band-Aids. The process is completely inadequate for the number of marriage failures. Without question, the Church's handling of divorce and remarriage is the single largest factor for the exit of members, and subsequently their children, from the Catholic Church. For many priests and lay people, it seems sad, if not cruel, to disregard older and simpler solutions for this dilemma in favor of a more discriminatory and complicated process such as the new annulment procedure.

## Retreat Master

In a retreat house in a New England state the director, Father Benedict, was particularly well known for being able to obtain annulments for failed marriages. Not only were people aware of this and would come to him, but several parish priests also directed their parishioners to seek help from him.

One spring I was giving a series of talks in the area and decided to go out to the retreat house to pay him a visit. We went for a walk around the lake, and I quizzed him regarding the secret of his success in procuring annulments. He laughed a little. "It was really not my doing. During one of the retreats I was expressing my concern about the severe problem for the Church in addressing marriage collapse today." He went on to add that he told his audience of women that many people just did not know how to get through all the paperwork and that if he took care of all the marriages that needed annulments that came into the retreat house, that ministry alone would require his full time. Afterward, three women came up to him and said that they had been looking for a ministry within the Church. One was an attorney, another a recorder in the county system, and the third a secretary. They agreed to give a minimum of six hours a week for those who needed help with the annulment process. The attorney was willing to visit the tribunal, secure the forms necessary for an annulment, and to explain the questions to those seeking an annulment. The county recorder said that she had easy access to resources for searching out documents not only in that area, but from any place in the world. The secretary promised to do the typing.

Whenever a couple was referred to him he would sit down and listen to them thoroughly, judging what was necessary to do in each case. They then proceeded to be interviewed by the county recorder in order to secure the necessary documents. The attorney was next in line for interviews. She explained the meaning of the process and the questions asked and recorded the conversation. This, in turn, was typed by the secretary in legal form. The person returned in approximately two weeks for the signing and the notarizing of the papers, which were then presented to the tribunal.

With a hearty laugh, the priest said that one of the tribunal members met him at a confirmation and remarked, "Benedict, you present the best marriage cases of anyone in the diocese."

He laughed again and said, "I told him, think nothing of it. It's a cinch. However, I know that when credits are given out in heaven for those who have given peace and redemption to people on earth, those three women will be among the greatest of them all. Last year we were complimented on processing seventy six annulments—more than any three parishes combined."

The retreat master looked out over the lake and added in a manner that indicated confidentiality, "I probably processed more pastorally than I did through the tribunal office. I would rather be part of the solution than part of the problem."

How can the Church continue to protect the permanence of marriage (which Protestant theologians and sociologists also support) yet, at the same time, minister to those who have been fractured by divorce? If the Church emphasizes one, the other seems to suffer.

## PREFERENCE PRINCIPLE THEORY

People can be trapped in life circumstances where it's damned if you do and damned if you don't, situations where both solutions are immoral to some degree. Throughout the centuries such situations were simply handled by choosing the lesser of the two evils. In moral theology this dilemma was addressed by the phrase "the principle of double effect." People had to choose an evil and more often than not agonized over which was the lesser.

Many individuals were faced with such a choice during the Vietnam war, not only those who were denied the status of conscientious objector and so had to choose between fighting, leaving the country, or going to jail, but also those who may not have wanted to work in industries related to armament and nuclear buildup but had large families to support. Another example is abortion where the life of the child threatens the life of the mother. Some are caught wondering whether to report an embezzlement or narcotics traffic when it could endanger their lives or the lives of other innocent parties. And in such cases even not making a choice, as the posters proclaim, is deciding.

For many centuries moral theology taught and was caught by the term "intrinsic evil." People were never supposed to do an intrinsically evil act under any circumstances. Certainly this, at times, produced heroic behavior. On the other hand, there was a very fine line between heroism and idiocy. The classic example was the case in which a person during World War II was faced with either telling a lie (intrinsic evil) and saving the life of Jews who were hidden in the basement of the house, or telling the truth and causing their death. Then the theory of intrinsic evil decreased in value.

This dilemma also applies to people who are in second marriages that are invalid or are supposed to be invalid, because they have a responsibility to their new spouse and certainly to children born of the second union. Such people are wrong if they stay in the marriage and wrong if they leave it. The premise of moral theologians who hold the preference principle theory is that no one should ever suffer religiously because of some human dilemma. This principle maintains that an individual caught in a dilemma seeks competent counsel if possible, prays, discerns, and makes the choice for the best, most responsible, and life-giving option. With this, the person accepts forgiveness for any wrong, gives gratitude to God for all that is good, and rejoices for being in "the state of grace."

The preference principle theory has given new clarity to pastoral situations for people who have to live a lifetime with the results of earlier human decisions. The cumbersome principle of double effect or, above all, the thought that there is no reconciliation for sin and its continuing effects, can now yield to a very simple and loving solution. The preference principle enunciates the redemptive insight that if a person can't go forward or backward religiously, then he or she can be confident that God will affirm whatever choice is made.

## IMPLEMENTATION OF THE THEORIES

### LAW AND COMMON SENSE

It is often said that law is without conscience. It often gets tangled up in itself and comes at cross-purposes. In fact, one of the laws in the canons of the Roman Catholic Church gives permission for a human being to set aside or violate the law in favor of good sense. This law is called *epikeia*. The Orthodox Church has a parallel in its concept of *oikonomia,* though it has a slightly different meaning. *Epikeia* might be translated, "The law doesn't make sense in this case, so use your good sense." *Oikonomia* might be translated, "The mercy of God supersedes the law." These are the laws of good judgment. The Roman Catholic Church officially recognizes the concept of *oikonomia* of the Orthodox Church knowing that its roots are firmly in Catholic tradition. *Oikonomia* allows a failed marriage to be taken before the Church leaders. If in their good judgment that marriage should be dissolved, a Church representative does so, and the individuals are allowed to be married in the Church a second time.

### EPIKEIA

In 1971 at Saint Joseph's Church in Los Angeles, an energetic, young Franciscan was visited one afternoon by couple who were both in their early seventies. They announced happily that they wanted to be married. The young priest was amazed that the seventy-year-old man had never been married before and that he was willing to embark upon a married life at his age.

His bride-to-be, of German descent, had been born in the Eastern sector of Berlin. After the occupation she was able to flee from the Russian-held Eastern sector to the American-held Western sector. From there she made her way to the United States. She had been estranged from her husband before her escape. Years later she received a letter from her cousin behind the Iron Curtain who informed her that her husband had committed suicide. After reading the letter and finding no need to retain it, she threw it away.

The young Franciscan congratulated them on their desire to marry in the Church, and said that he did not foresee any difficulty; however, he would check it. With their permission, he left the parlor and phoned the tribunal. He was informed to get the marriage certificate and the death certificate and he could proceed with the marriage. The priest returned to the parlor, took down the necessary information, and sent off a request with $10 to cover return postage and to encourage a response. He bade the elderly couple goodbye.

Months later they returned and asked for the priest. He was summoned and sat down in the parlor with them. The priest recalled the case and checked his files. No response from East Germany had come in. He informed them of the lack of documentation.

The man and woman looked at each other, and she turned to the priest and said, "Father, we're not getting any younger. We do not have too much time to enjoy each other. We cannot wait too long. Besides, Father, you will never receive a certificate from East Germany. They do not issue anything."

The priest shook his head. He remembered that he had requested certificates before from East Germany and had never received any. He asked to be excused and went to his office phone. He called the tribunal and explained the situation. The tribunal member who had taken the call told the priest that they needed that death certificate before the marriage could be performed in the Church. Though a bit awed by the possible finality of the decision of the tribunal member, the priest confronted the issue by reiterating exactly what the elderly lady had said.

"I'm sorry," came the voice from the tribunal member. "We cannot help her until you get the document."

Attempting to be gracious, the Franciscan said, "Thank you, Father, for your trouble." He hung up the phone. Furious at what he had just encountered, he left his office, passed by the parlor where the elderly couple were chatting, and went inside the door of the monastery. He walked into the interior office where priests often gather to receive their mail and messages and found the pastor sitting there.

The pastor had received his degree in canon law from the Gregorianum in Rome. The young priest explained the situation to the pastor, using angry words about it being unfair. What was he to do?

"Settle down, Anthony," came the gentle response. "The tribunal is a legal procedure that needs documents to function. The tribunal member was responding correctly—he cannot help you."

With a smile and looking straight at the young associate, the venerable pastor said, "Have you ever heard of *epikeia?* The tribunal can't help them. You must."

The associate looked at him and said, "You mean I can perform that marriage?"

The response was, "According to *epikeia,* pastoral judgment and decision. These people are covered by the law but cannot be helped by it. That is *epikeia.* "

The associate turned, walked out into the parlor, and asked the elderly couple when they would like to be married. The response was surprising but understandable.

"Right now, if we could! We already have the license."

The young associate found himself saying, "Would you like to get married at the main altar or the side altar?"

When Jacqueline Kennedy married Aristotle Onassis, she could not do so in her Roman Catholic tradition; Onassis had been married and divorced. However Onassis, an Orthodox, had his first marriage dissolved by *oikonomia.* Therefore he could marry Jacqueline Kennedy in his Orthodox Church tradition in a sacramental way. Since he was a person in good standing in the Orthodox Church, when he went to the Roman Catholic Eucharist, he could legitimately receive Communion. However, by the same code of law, Jacqueline, a Roman Catholic, could not receive Communion. For the laws of the Church to make sense, *oikonomia* and *epikeia* will always have to be present. Interestingly enough, when these laws of good judgment are exercised by an individual, the person is often censured or even punished by the institution as though it could be the only dispenser of good sense.

## INDISSOLUBILITY

Jesus taught the indissolubility of marriage. The Church first taught the indissolubility of marriage, then the indissolubility of all sacramental marriages, and now teaches the indissolubility of all marriages.

Regarding the first statement above, the greater number of theologians agree that Jesus taught the indissolubility of marriage. The concept of sacramentality was not developed for another eleven hundred years. Jesus' reference must have been to all marriages. Yet the Church made exceptions with the Pauline and Petrine privileges. This obviously demonstrates that Church practice saw Jesus' pronouncement on indissolubility as applying to marriage in general but not necessarily to each marriage.

Regarding the second statement above, Church teaching and practice are not always the same. The Church has always taught indissolubility of marriage. However, in practice before A.D. 1100 the Church permitted remarriage after the failure of a Christian marriage. The Church also allowed remarriage after the failure of a nonsacramental marriage by using the Pauline and Petrine privileges. Also the annulment process itself allows two baptized married people to enter a second marriage because the first marriage was not sacramental.

The official Church teaching on the Council of Trent is:

Cardinal Huizing has stressed the fact that before Trent there was little or no truly structured canonical legislation of marriage. The International Theological Commission, in the text of its *Propositions on the Doctrine of Christian Marriage* published in 1978, recognizes the fact that even at the time of Trent, theological opinion on the subject of indissolubility was not unanimous. . . . The document explicitly states: "It cannot be said then, that the Council had the intention of solemnly defining marriage's indissolubility as a truth of faith."[25]

If we took all the councils of the Church and tried to organize their teachings we would not, then, have a unified teaching of indissolubility for every marriage.

## INTERNAL FORUM

Saint Augustine once said, "The Church has many that God does not; God has many that the Church does not." Those who are juridical, logical, and structural don't care for this insight of the early doctor of the Church. Those who are intuitive, philosophical, humanitarian, and evangelical, usually respond "how true!" In a legalistic culture where we do a simple credit card transaction in triplicate, we produce legalistic people. We don't care for Pascal's famous saying, "The heart has reasons that reason knows not of." The Roman Catholic concepts of the external forum and the internal forum are highly legalistic.

"Forum" is a Latin word that in ancient Roman times indicated the open area where business was transacted, like a public square. The Catholic concept of external forum is that domain concerned with what is just and what is necessary to regulate the movement of a community as a whole. The internal forum has to do with what is just for the individual. When clergy invoke internal forum to minister to parishioners they are to do so in a personal manner with charity, equity, and gentleness.[26]

The principal purpose of the Church is to help people be aware of the salvation through Jesus Christ. When the Church does this by proclamation and legislation for all the members as one body, this is called external forum. But in a community of hundreds, to say nothing of thousands (as in a parish) and even millions, Catholics become aware of their salvation only on a personal, individual basis as the laws or norms apply to their particular case; this is internal forum. Since the Church is an institution, by its very nature its legislation has always preferred the external rather than the internal forum.

External and internal fora are methods through which an individual can recognize his or her full accord with the grace of God within the community. Every time clergy exercise either, they should be careful to give rationale for the direction given so that the individual does not think the ministering procedure is some type of magic wand.

The exercise of the internal forum by either clergy or laity usually takes a deeper faith and more maturity than exercise of the external forum. Because it is personal, the responsibility for exercising it is assumed by the individual and not by Church hierarchy or law. For this reason the internal forum also goes under the name of "good conscience," "good faith," or "pastoral care." The internal forum honors the personal conscience of an individual—his or her honest appreciation of a life situation.

Chief Justice Holmes once said that the law of the land is not expected to be humane, only logical. Fortunately, Church law is much more humane than civil law. *Epikeia* is the law of the Church that acknowledges that not every case is covered by the law. It is the Church's official way of saying, "This is the law; now use good sense." Ironically, this is often very threatening to the highly structured and legalistic people sometimes found in chancery offices and older clerical circles. If priests and laity individually used good sense, there would be no need for control by the organizational authorities. It is interesting to know that the Church law of *epikeia* admits with those of a more charismatic and evangelical bent that the greatness of God cannot always be systematized.

This sensitive protection of individuals, *epikeia,* was contained in the 1917 code of canon law (Canons 196 and 1512).[27] As a consequence, many of the bishops of the United States who had missionary areas in their dioceses told their priests to bypass the tribunal system for the uneducated of their diocese. This applied to all the minority groups, but particularly to Indians, Hispanics, and blacks. After the disruption of World War I unresolvable marriage entanglements became more apparent even among the educated. There were multiple marriages, the disappearance of spouses, and quick marriages in foreign lands or behind the Iron Curtain, all of which could not be helped by the tribunal process. However, as some tribunals became more efficient, tension grew between those clerics exercising the internal forum while disregarding the external forum. On April 11, 1973, a clarification of this came officially from the Congregation of the Doctrine of the Faith in a directive communicated to the bishops around the world and signed by Cardinal Seper. While reaffirming the Church's teaching on indissolubility, the closing paragraph reemphasized the necessity of pastoral care and compassion:

In regard to admission of the sacraments, local bishops are asked on the one hand to stress observance of current discipline, and on the other hand to take care that pastors of souls exercise special care to seek out those who are living in an irregular union by applying to the solution of such cases, in addition to other rightful means, the Church's approved practice in the internal forum.[28]

In typical legalistic fashion, the bishops of the United States asked for a further clarification of the words "Church's approved practice." The following was sent to Archbishop Bernardin from the Sacred Congregation in Rome:

I would like to state now that this phrase must be understood in the context of traditional, moral theology. These couples may be allowed to receive the sacraments on two conditions, that they try to live according to the demands of Christian moral principles and that they receive the sacraments in churches in which they are not known so that they will not create any scandal.[29]

No mention was made about the previous marriage being valid or invalid. The directive was simply to people of good faith.

The principle of internal forum, then, recognizes the divine right of people to live in the grace of God. A priest should accompany its use with an explanation of the Church's tradition of understanding and mercy, but point out that the one using it personally assumes responsibility for it.[30] For that reason internal forum can be exercised in or outside the framework of sacramental confession. Confession is often used because its cleansing power aids in relieving a faith-filled person of some of the ugliness of a failed marriage or divorce. Because of the "seal of confession" (absolute secrecy), some priests like to use the protection of the sacrament of reconciliation for both himself and the individual in case some righteous individual challenges a remarried person's right to participation in the sacraments.

Many of the pastoral directives concerning the internal forum state limitations about it. It is usually stated that by using internal forum a priest cannot validate a second marriage while the spouse of the first marriage is still alive. Such a statement is limited and in some cases incorrect. It is obviously not a validation equivalent to one done by use of the external forum. But if the first marriage was truly invalid and the second marriage could not be processed in the external forum, it certainly would be.

Another limitation is usually expressed: that the internal forum cannot be used as permission for a previously married person whose spouse is still living to remarry in the Catholic Church. That, too, can be incorrect. Both the old code of canon law (Canon

1098) and the new code (Canon 1116) clearly state that if a person has a right to get married before God but cannot get access to proper authority within one month, they can use any authority, even just two witnesses. This is sometimes called the "desert island" canon. It is often used when two Roman Catholics find themselves in an area without priests because of political persecution or remoteness. Some canon lawyers also apply this canon to the case where a couple lives next door to the rectory and has a right to get married before God but the priest refuses to care for them. Such a marriage, by the code, is in the Catholic Church.

Another stated limitation of the internal forum is that it is not permissible for a priest to perform any kind of public or private ceremony that has the appearance of an official marriage ceremony or validation. Because a large number of Roman Catholics have been trained to think that marriages are only valid when performed in a church building, emotionally they will not feel married unless there is some type of recognition within the church building before a priest or deacon. *Epikeia* could certainly be used in those cases where the previous marriage took place several years before and very far away. Scandal is not likely. Why forbid a blessing for the children of God when we bless cars, guns, and dogs? Furthermore, a priest may say a Mass for anyone. How can the divorced and remarried be excluded?

In most cases, in the internal forum, the priest is dealing with Catholics who have already been remarried by a civil or non-Catholic ceremony. In these cases a blessing for peace of conscience can easily be facilitated. In the cases where an annulment is not possible or recommended and the Catholic party or parties have not yet remarried, caution must be taken by the priest both on behalf of loyalty to the Church's proclamation of indissolubility of marriage and scandal of the Catholic community. If the priest signs the second marriage license he is flaunting the Church's process of annulment in this culture. If there is a large church wedding without an annulment, the Catholic community will be completely confused. Most priests who are conscientious about the official teaching on remarriage in this Catholic culture and attuned to the often agonizing need of the devout member to be blessed before the altar have the couple marry quietly before the justice of peace and then have the immediate family present for the blessing in the church. This seems to be a graceful solution for honoring the institutional and the personal. Such a solution is a small concession on the part of the Catholic party; about seventy percent of the Roman Catholics throughout the world marry civilly first and then go to the church for the blessing.

A father-son relationship existed between a fifty-five-year-old bishop and a thirty-year-old priest, Father Dan, in one of the dioceses of the Southwest. The bishop was a now-graying man who had spent his lifetime in chancery offices and tribunals. As a newly ordained priest, the bishop had been intelligent and gifted with common sense; he was tall and stately, gentle and handsome. From the very beginning he was slated to go places in the hierarchy, and he did. He was a man who made the institution attractive.

On the other hand, Father Dan was zesty and occasionally spicy in his language. He rarely wore clerical garb and exhibited a free spirit by doing very "unpriestly" things such as parachuting, rafting down the Colorado, and occasionally acting in the local theater. Dan was a reader of theology and unusually versatile with different age groups, a devout celebrant at the altar, and a joy to be around. Those who knew the relationship between the bishop and Father Dan philosophized that the former longed to have the freedom and simplicity of the latter.

On one occasion, at a social for priests after a golf tournament, the bishop, Father Dan, and other priests were gathered around the hors d'oeuvre table. The subject of annulments came up. With utter simplicity and clarity, Dan commented that the legal aspects, the forms and lawyers, did not help the Church appear pastoral. With his typical enthusiasm Dan described how he took parties through the annulment process so that they did not feel that they were on trial; rather, they were searching to heal a bad memory. With utter candor he admitted that he used an equally good pastoral process because he wanted the Church to be more of a sanctuary than a courtroom.

A few of the priests gulped out of surprise and a few nervously went for the hors d'oeuvres in front of them. So there would be no confusion about his episcopal policy, with a drink in one hand and the index finger of the other officially pointing up, the bishop said, "I've heard that, Dan." And looking him straight in the eye as the finger came down in accusation, "If I ever catch you, I will suspend you."

With the instant love so typical of him, Father Dan pointed his finger at the bishop and said, "I think you are officially telling me to do it right so I don't get caught."

A few priests rolled their eyes as though they were praying they might evaporate from the uncomfortable conversation. The bishop looked stunned and gracefully changed the subject with the remark, "Dan, I hope someday you are made a bishop, and I wish ten of your kind on you."

Dan tilted his head back in laughter and responded, "Hey, what have I done to deserve that curse?"

Customs vary from diocese to diocese and parish to parish and priest to priest with regard to the implementation of internal forum. Some feel free to assure people of the right to Communion within the sacrament of penance, others speak to them in the parlor, and still others take them to the church to offer prayers for their marriage. Others offer a Mass for them and some of their family in the church, and even still others invite a Protestant minister or a justice of the peace to the church to receive their vows and afterward offer a Mass for them.

In stark contrast to the ordinary use of the internal forum, in 1976, Bishop Dozier of Memphis, Tennessee, performed a general absolution for divorced and remarried Catholics who had not gone through the regular tribunal procedures. This caused a great deal of controversy because it seemed to resemble the magic wand solution. There were some, both clerical and lay, who felt that this form of general amnesty undermined the Church's regular position on the indissolubility of marriage. It was interesting that higher Church officials disagreed with the content of the bishop's proclamation but not with his right to exercise the power.

PASTORAL SOLUTION

Since it is very difficult to determine in many disintegrated marrital relationships whether, according to the annulment process, there was really sufficient ability at the time of the marriage or not, many canon lawyers have suggested an ad hoc commission to give direction to the parties on the parish level with the right to appeal to the diocese. The board would counsel the parties toward helping them objectively evaluate their personal convictions about the invalidity of the marriage. Such a committee would urge confessors to advise their penitents to follow a well-informed conscience even if this would be in conflict with external legislation.[31]

There is an obvious conflict between the Church's official teaching of the absolute indissolubility of marriage and the pastoral practice of caring for the divorced and/or remarried. There are many canon lawyers and even more moral theologians who consider the Church's insistence on annulment through the external forum immoral. It is immoral because of all the Roman Catholics who appeal to the Church's representatives for annulment, it is estimated that less than ten percent will even be heard. Though the personnel of the tribunals has vastly improved in the last decade, it is still replete with part-time workers and people without professional training. Because of the Church's insistence, at least in the English-speaking world, on presenting the annulment process as the official form of reconciliation allowing a second marriage, thousands upon thousands of Catholics separate themselves from the Church since they see no hope. Furthermore, in the process of annulment it is demonstrated that one or both parties were incapable of committing to marriage at the time of the wedding. Yet the granting of the annulment permits both to remarry, although they may not be any more capable now. In some rare cases the tribunal requires psychological approval of one party before a second marriage. This is called a vetitum. However, there are few of these compared to the vast number of pronouncements of inadequacy.

In all fairness it would be exaggerating to say that the annulment process is immoral. The insistence on the process in every case may well be immoral. To say that the annulment process was the only solution in helping nearly nine million Roman Catholics in second marriages return to sacramental practice would certainly be immoral. The process would collapse addressing even ten percent of that population. This evaluation is not contained in scripture. It is a human evaluation. The Church itself has had to change some of these evaluations lest a solution for one era becomes counterproductive in another.

## Deanary Meeting

At a deanary meeting of priests in Detroit, a tribunal member presented the new annulment forms and the process the archdiocese was then going to use. The explanation was well received.

Just before the meeting adjourned, an energetic priest held up his hand, was recognized, and stood up to address the priests. He asked the twenty-five priests present the question, "Could any of us say that we have never advised a pastoral solution for a couple?" Some of the elderly priests sat immobile. Others were looking around, and some of them said, "I can't say that."

The priest continued. "Apparently, then, all of us have done pastoral solutions. Let me ask another question. How many of you, in doing a pastoral solution, feel that you are working without the permission of the Church or even feel that you are doing something secretive and in doing so fear 'getting caught'?" Ninety-five percent of the hands went up.

"Isn't that interesting? Most of us feel guilty for doing what the Church permits."

He went on to ask, "How many of you would welcome a workshop on performing pastoral solutions? We could get a theologian, a canon lawyer, and a moral theologian to give us explicit directions like the ones we have for the annulment process." The speaker then turned to the member of the tribunal and said, "I know of a theologian, a canon lawyer, and a moral theologian who would be willing to give us this workshop. Would you be willing to get the bishop's permission for this?"

The tribunal member responded regretfully. "I don't think the bishop will go for it, but I do think it is a good idea. We can ask." Permission for the workshop was later denied.

On all levels the Church has to rethink its position on marriage theology. Cardinal Huizing has complained that canon law has become the theology of marriage within the Church. This is a mistake since such legal norms are not the only ones justified theologically. One of the greatest systematic theologians of this era, Edward Schillebeeckx, complains that the Church is essentially a public community, yet the internal forum, while certainly merciful, is clandestine, which contradicts the very meaning of the sacraments. The laws of the Church should follow its theology and dogma, not vice versa. So Bernard Haring, another Church theologian, bluntly states that the Church should rethink its concept of the indissolubility of marriage. Charles Curran, a moral theologian at the Catholic University of America, in an address to the Canon Law Society of America, argued that the Catholic Church should change its teaching on the absolute indissolubility of marriage.[32]

When the internal forum is used individually, it can provide a profound religious experience for divorced persons. Such individuals can be introduced into the rich heritage of the Catholic tradition and can be led to a deeper appreciation of the Church, which has never flippantly disregarded the words of Jesus with regard to marriage but has been perplexed in handling the human condition. Such persons can also become aware of the element of the mystery in proclaiming indissolubility, which they would certainly want for a second marriage. Divorced persons of the Western culture could also be introduced to the more profound spiritual insights in the Eastern concepts of consummation, covenant, levels of marriage, *oikonomia*, and of the different kinds of death of a marriage. This faith enrichment may lead many to make the first responsible decision for which they, and not Church organization, will be personally accountable before God.

When faced with putting religion into practice in the actual journey of life, a divorced person may have to acknowledge that he or she is interpreting childhood teachings as a child. Often that teaching was inadequate or positively incorrect. An individual might finally give up the broken record of "what Sister said" and "what Father said," put aside the things of a child, and grow up in the Lord.

To repeat from the introduction, the following conclusions can be drawn from the evidence of Church theory, declarations, and practice:

- A divorced Catholic can never be prohibited from receiving Communion.
- A sincere Catholic remarried "outside the Church" can never be prohibited from receiving Communion. With competent clerical or lay help (even this book) a person could make a decision about a previous marriage and terminate its religious binding force. Even if this determination is absent, according to the explicit declaration of the Sacred Congregation in Rome (March 21, 1975), a remarried Catholic could be admitted to the sacraments.
- A second marriage can be sacred in the Roman Catholic Church without an annulment of the first.

# 5. Forming a Conscience: The Challenge to Live as Mature Christians

One of the most exasperating things about working in the ministry to the divorced and remarried is not only the folklore or misconceptions people still carry around, but their failure to grow up in their faith and make responsible choices as they must do in other areas of life.

A man in New Hampshire was having difficulty with the changes in the Church. In the midst of his complaints, a priest asked him what his field of employment was. The man quickly responded that it was math and computer science. The priest also asked him about his education. The man admitted that he had a doctorate in both fields., The priest then inquired if there had been any changes in the field of computer technology. Without hesitation, the response was that it was one of the most rapidly changing fields in America. The priest also asked him if he had to read and attend workshops in order to stay abreast of things. The man confessed that he constantly did that. Then the priest asked him why he did not want to do the same with his own religion. He immediately responded that when he went to Church he wanted some stability—to have things just like his mother taught him. He did not see why the Church had to change.

This is probably the very core of why divorced and remarried people do not participate fully in the sacrament. As a preacher said so accurately when paraphrasing Saint Paul's Letter to the Corinthians, "When I was a child I used to talk like a child, think like a child, and reason like a child. Now that I'm an adult, I talk like a child, think like a child, and reason like a child." Such is the progress of millions of Catholics in their faith. For many of them religious growth ended in grade school or high school.

People often become religiously mature due to a crisis in life. Yet without such a catalyst maturity of human development is noticeably lacking in many aspects of religious practice, as well as in the lives of many religious people.

Jesus himself speaks about the failure to make mature judgments in religious matters in, for example, the parables of the talents and the vineyard. He also says near the end of his life, "I have much more to tell you, but you cannot bear it now. When he comes, however, being the Spirit of truth he will guide you to all truth." (John 16:12-13)

This need for growth in knowledge and responsibility in moral decisions was given world press at the Nuremberg trials. In case after case, it was found inadmissable for a person to have let a higher authority decide his or her conscience; full punishment was due those who committed crimes because they were "told to."

On the other hand, these trials revealed individuals who stood up to both Church and state to proclaim error and sin. Without question, many of them suffered opposition and punishment. Nevertheless, assuming responsibility of conscience before God made them saints.

Interestingly enough, investigators who have studied the faith intensity of religious people have found that those who are fearful of forming their own conscience in their religious practice are individuals who have a greater faith in "rote observance" of ritual than they have in a personal relationship with God. A kinder interpretation would be that their personal relationship with God is highly dependent on religious directives and laws. Those who participate very little in religious structure and ritual, but who assume a personal relationship with God, have very few problems in formulating their conscience. Another observation is that if a person agonizes in heart and mind in formulating his or her conscience in a moral decision, it most likely reveals the presence of a severe God. If a person formulates his or her conscience in moral matters in a spirit of trust, joy, and confidence, it most likely reveals a loving, caring God.

## BACK TO JESUS

Jesus gave us very few specific lists of moral and immoral actions; rather he gave general guiding principles. He said, "You will live in my love if you keep my commandments." His commandments were only two: "You shall love the Lord your God with your whole heart, your whole soul, and with all your mind . . . [and] love your neighbor as yourself." If all of the actions of human behavior were put on a scale of 0 to 1000, it might be said that he gave explicit directions about .005 of them. Evaluations of human actions are almost totally humanly formulated and the ensuing morality may be called humanmade. Probably the fastest way to encourage Roman Catholics to make responsible moral decisions would be to have them take a course on how "the Church" makes statements and decisions on what is moral and what is immoral. It is almost certain the Baltimore Catechism Catholics would want to become part of the decision-making process.

The average Roman Catholic learns that in the consideration of what constitutes a sin, a person has to know whether an action is mortally or venially sinful (serious or light) and has to will it. Because many have never gone beyond the first catechism, they have never realized that there are volumes and volumes of Church-approved disputes on which sins are grave or light, many of them acknowledging it is impossible to know. Beside on the quality of an action, a great deal of dispute ensued over the years over the different kinds of ignorance and compulsions that freed people from culpability in a particular action. The imaginations of the moralists in this area were particularly fertile, which produced even more volumes on moral options. In fact, the Church has whole schools of thought ranging from the very strict to the very lenient— all of which can be bonafide in the eyes of the teaching Church. New moral evaluations have constantly gone on in the Church, as in the case of slavery, usury, war, capital punishment, fasting, and many other issues. New circumstances require new solutions.

Many theologians have difficulty with even the simplistic categories of mortal and venial sin. It is an arbitrary evalution (it is not contained in Scripture) and one that keeps Catholics from responding responsibly to the teachings of the Second Vatican

Council. To many moralists, unless the Church officially changes this evaluation, scores of Catholics will still think people go to hell over a hot dog on Friday or are damned for all eternity for missing Mass on a Sunday. In the eyes of many, this is moral irresponsibility that demands some radical change.

The Catholic Theological Society of America has suggested that a fresh start be given to the moral evaluation of human actions. It defines a mortal sin as a direct act of hatred against God, a serious sin as any action that causes serious harm to oneself or another, and a venial sin as one that causes minor harm to oneself or another. This change would demand that each human action receive a new appraisal with reference to past evaluations and the knowledge of new realities and that there be a conscious interaction about this in the Christian community.

## APPLICATION

All of this is applicable to those who are divorced and remarried, both according to the old moral evaluation and certainly the new. Was it a mortal sin to leave the marriage or stay in it? How culpable was a person in the eventual demise of the marriage relationship? Who determined divorce and remarriage as the unforgivable sin of Scripture? Is that agreed upon by all the schools of thought approved by the Church?

If a person is following a decision made by human conscience that deprives him or her of Church practice, who's conscience is that? It has to be somebody's conscience. Why not the person's own?

Time and time again in pastoral practice, a sensitive person in ministry will ask remarried individuals what they think God would say if they went before the Almighty that night. Thousands have said, "I would have no problems with God. All my problems are with the Church." Maybe it's not the Church either, but this righteous person's interpretation of "what the Church teaches."

What does it take to make people accept the fact that it is before God that they will be responsible in conscience decisions? Church practices are meant to be a reflection of that essential relationship. It is not up to some priest or father or mother or anyone else to decide another's personal intimacy with God in the sacraments.

So strongly rooted is this concept in Church teaching that even Saint Thomas Aquinas writes, ". . . anyone upon whom the ecclesiastical authority, in ignorance of true facts, imposes a demand that offends against his clear conscience, should perish in excommunication rather than violate his conscience."[32]

The Vatican II documents emphasize that people are to follow an informed conscience. Perhaps making conscience decisions in this issue of divorce and remarriage will bring Catholics to a more mature faith and to a deeper realization of God's love through the Church. An individual might begin by internalizing the fact that he or she is the Church as part of the people of God. And the Church, because it is made up of people, must struggle for the truth, which is part of becoming holy; forming a conscience for an individual can be a holy process. Ordinary Catholics must again and again be reminded that as part of the faith community they are part of the teaching Church. A dramatic example of this whole maturing process might be seen in the making of conscience decisions about birth control. A similar maturing process with regard to divorce and remarriage might well be an answer to the mass alienation of divorced Catholics from the practice of faith in a Church of which they are an integral part.

## TWENTIETH-CENTURY GROWTH

If centuries could have stages of development similar to those in humans, the twentieth century might have the following description. At the beginning of the century, the Catholic laity might be described as infants, or sheep, to be led and cared for. With the growing popularity of parochial schools in the twenties and thirties, the laity moved into puberty. During this stage, they knew a few religious answers "by heart" (really "by head") and even quoted what Sister said rather than the priest in authority. In the late forties and fifties, Catholic Action moved the laity into assuming some responsibility in religious decisions along with the priest. In fact, Pius XII defined Catholic Action as "the participation of the laity in the work of the priest." These were the teenage or early adolescent years.

After Vatican II in the sixties, the laity might be described as being in late adolescence, for rebellion and anger were common. The Church teaching from that council called the laity to assume responsibility in ministry because they were baptized and not because they were directed or requested to by the pastor or other clergy. This change made the authority structure horizontal, not pyramidal, and left not only the laity but also the religious personnel at a loss as to how to manage this new-found responsibility. In fact, the changes from the Second Vatican Council resulted in the fourth greatest exit of religious in the history of the Catholic Church, ranking alongside the plague, the Protestant Reformation, and the French Revolution.

Many of the lay people who were taught to "pay, pray, and obey" did so with religious devotion, but they learned by rote and not by thinking; thinking was rationalizing. Many were devastated when official sainthood was taken away from Christopher and destiny was no longer jeopardized by eating a hot dog on Friday. These changes, though shocking, were no doubt providential. Once the adolescent anger abated, both religious and lay who remained faithful to Church practice saw it evolve from ritual by habit or demand to ritual with meaning and worship.

Christopher was not a historical person who lived in a certain century, but rather a type of saint who lived in every century, one who sought, found, and carried Christ. The custom of not eating meat on Friday, very recent in Church history and known by probably less than twenty percent of the Roman Catholic population at the turn of this century, returned to a religious act one chose to perform as a remembrance of one's redemption.

The demand for mature faith was not over. *Humanae Vitae,* the encyclical addressing human life and birth control, resulted in the greatest loss of Church membership in the early seventies. The Catholic laity of this century then came into the young adult stage; some even matured to adulthood. Surveys at the end of the seventies and the beginning of the eighties indicated that both priests and laity acknowledged the official teaching of the Church and yet decided according to personal conscience in the birth control debate. Growing up is proverbially painful. Even in a tradition of suffering and sorrow, as in Catholicism, pain is not always welcomed.

The reason for the greatest loss of Church membership in the eighties is the Church's best known position on divorce and remarriage. Again, it is painful on many levels. Not only does the Church loose many people who are directly affected by divorce, but it also loses their children and their children's children. This issue may be the real challenge in coming to a responsible and mature faith among religious and lay Catholics in our century. Let's look at the birth control issue as an example.

## BIRTH CONTROL REVISITED

On July 29, 1968, the theological world was rocked by the encyclical *Humanae Vitae*. Though the title of the encyclical directed its message toward human life, the birth control issue thundered forth to dominate many messages in its text. Perhaps the faith response to this encyclical may have a salient parallel in the faith response to the issue of divorce and remarriage in our decade.

At the time of the publication of the encyclical, a major theologian said that discussion would ensue less about birth control itself than about the role of the teaching Church in the Catholic faith. What we have then are two different issues: the teaching Church and what the Church is teaching, which, in this case, concerns birth control.

## THE TEACHING CHURCH

It should be recalled that at the beginning of this century the Church's teaching was received as nearly absolute. Infallibility of the pope had been defined in 1870. The Church was still defensive —other religions were heretical and modernism needed to be sternly addressed. A succession of genius popes held the chair of Saint Peter. Perhaps one of the greatest geniuses of all time was Pius XII (1939–1958). Churchill praised him as probably the most brilliant mind of his era. He had three doctorates by the time he was twenty-three years old, wrote sixty-six volumes on social justice issues, and never contradicted himself once. John Kennedy said he would read his encyclicals over any sociological analyses because they were so brilliant and went beyond the boundaries of a single nation. Because of these factors, everything that came from the Vatican took on the appearance of divine revelation. This was known as "creeping infallibility," even though in actual fact only two infallible statements have ever been made. Time and time again, religion teachers stated that the pope could make mistakes in everyday pronouncements, but the overwhelming power of the papal position overrode any awareness of that among the majority of Roman Catholics. Many of the brilliant social encyclicals were ignored, but there was virtually never any open opposition to any of the papal statements until *Humanae Vitae.* Controversy was then unleashed. Papal statements since that time are in a new historical era.

## HISTORICAL SETTING OF BIRTH CONTROL

Strangely enough, it was the work of both missionaries and medicine that brought about a serious concern for world overpopulation. Attempting to control death brought about a concern for birth control. The Malthusian theory of the last century brought about an awareness of the geometrical increase in population. Margaret Sanger, a nurse who worked in the inner city, began to decry the human misery and death caused by indiscriminate birth. Religions were unanimous in reaffirming the value of life. Sociologists spoke of tribal survival and enough people to work the land in underdeveloped countries. At first both Catholic and Protestant religions were united against the birth control movement. Such opposition even swelled in overpopulated cities. The Great Depression broke loose in November of 1929 causing vast unemployment and starvation. In August of 1930, the Lambreth Conference of the Episcopalians reluctantly conceded to the position that birth control can be a moral choice. In December of the same year, the papal encyclical signed by Pius XI *Casti Canubii* reiterated that procreation was the primary purpose for marriage. After this encyclical, the Protestant churches were nearly unanimous in lining up with the Lambreth statement. From this time on, on the issue of birth control Catholics and Protestants were sharply divided.

The pain of the Depression throughout the world pressured Catholicism to devise some measures to control birth when having a child was either physically dangerous or morally difficult. The medical profession began to notice in the early part of the century that women were fertile and infertile at different times during the month. Refraining from intercourse at fertile times—called the rhythm method—seemed to be a solution for Catholics. Based on the scientific approach of Saint Thomas Aquinas, abstaining from intercourse would not be considered as an abuse of the act, whereas using something artificial would be. But because the medical profession was unable to specify the times of infertility with accuracy, the rhythm method lost its credibility as a solution for controlling birth. It was unaffectionately known as "Vatican roulette."

More people began taking personal responsibility in the forties and fifties through the work of Catholic Action. Among the different forms of Catholic Action was the Catholic Family Movement. Their motto was "think, judge, and act." Gradually they led married couples to think, judge, and respond; there was more to marriage than just procreation. Soon they were reminding Church leaders that people married primarily out of love for one another and only secondarily to have children. The voices of married couples were being heard by theologians. Bernard Haring, who held the principal chair of moral theology in Rome, took a sabbatical to live on a family level in order to write a more integrated theology of marriage.

## GROUND SWELL

At the end of the fifties the United Nations became involved in population problems. Without qualification, birth control was one of their solutions in overpopulated areas of the world.

The reigning pontiff Pope John XXIII was an individual unafraid of controversy and a supreme seeker of truth. Acknowledging that birth control was not a revealed matter in Scripture, he called a conference to study overpopulation; birth control was a subsidiary issue. The first small committee of theologians, when asked for their results, answered that they were not sure. They needed more information from experts in other fields. Then began the entrance of people from the different sciences—ethnology, sociology, medicine, psychology, and demography. Before the conference was completed, Pope John died; his successor, Pope Paul VI, continued the conference. By this time $1.5 million had been spent gathering these resource people in the search of truth. The members of the conference had obviously seen the possibility of repositioning the Church's statement on birth control.

During this time the world was becoming frighteningly aware of the limitations of the scientific approach to life; nuclear annihilation loomed as a possibility. The personalistic and holistic viewpoint took prominence for survival's sake. This also influenced theology. The mechanistic approach to analyzing human actions crumbled before the more holistic models expounded by Saint Bonaventure of the Franciscan school. Without question, this was the overriding tone of all the documents that came from the Second Vatican Council.

The council documents spoke explicity of responsible parenting that included looking not only at conception but the ability to raise a child to full adulthood. It seemed obvious to most that artificial birth control would be the manner in which couples would be fulfilling this responsibility since, in many instances, abstinence from intercourse was not an option for a noticeable population of married couples.

At this time a famous Catholic doctor wrote a book, *The Time Has Come,* showing the necessity for artificial birth control. Many priests in touch with the needs of their parishioners began helping individuals formulate their own consciences about it. The mood, especially in theological communities, was that the Church would almost certainly alter its teaching concerning artificial birth control.

This was further enhanced when the report of the commission called by Pope John XXIII and continued by Pope Paul VI was finally finished and presented. Eighty-five percent of the commission saw the possibility of using artificial birth control, with the exception of the IUD because of the possibility of abortion. This part of the commission felt that they were in perfect harmony with the statements made in the Vatican documents on family life. Only fifteen percent were opposed to artificial birth control, basing their determination on the moral theology of Saint Thomas Aquinas. The drama reached a crescendo when the *National Catholic Reporter* published the entire report from the papal commission a short time after it was presented to the pope. Theologians, heirarchy, and priests simply waited for the manner in which artificial birth control would be approved.

A year and a half later, in 1968, theologians, hierarchy, priests, and laity sat in shock as Paul VI agreed with the fifteen percent and continued the hard line of condoning no artificial means of birth control.

Chaos followed. A tidal wave of shock and disbelief swept

through clergy and laity alike. It reversed the collegiality so deeply sponsored by the Second Vatican Council. After the publication of the encyclical *Humanae Vitae,* Pope Paul VI asked for support by the bishops, theologians, and clergy, but the impact was too great. Countless numbers of priests who were involved in Church marriage and family programs left the ministry. Surveys illustrated graphically that the greatest loss of membership from the Church, especially in the United States, was due to the encyclical *Humanae Vitae.* One of the major theologians in the United States admitted years later that the papal pronouncement was so overwhelming and outrageous that he had to go into seclusion for nearly a year. For almost five years after the publication, the Catholic community was divided into those who were staunchly "in defense of the faith" (the encyclical), those who gave up and left, a small portion who found some refuge in the advent of "the pill," and a group who felt they had the courage to make up their own minds.

When the smoke of emotion cleared, a modified perspective on the papal statement began to surface. It was recalled that at the very publication of the encyclical, Paul VI had stated explicitly, "may the lively debate roused by our encyclical lead to a better knowledge of God's will." Little did he know, no doubt, of how people would come to the knowledge of God's will. Because of this statement, Monsignor Lambruschini, a professor of moral theology at the Lateran Theological Seminary in Rome, announced the encyclical with the words:

This is not infallible. . . . We now have an official teaching on this matter. The rule is not irreformable. It is up to theologians to debate and expand all the moral aspects involved; and if, for instance, some principle should become overwhelmingly accepted in the Church, contraception may even be approved.

Numerous outstanding moral theologians of the Church dissented from the statement of the encyclical such as Rahner, Haring, Schillebeeckz, Jansens, Burkhart, McCormick, and Curran. None of these were asked to retract their positions when called on by various papal delegates. Within two years of the publication of the encyclical eight major episcopates throughout the world, while supporting the encyclical as an ideal for everyone, acknowledged the varying degrees in which people would be able to follow it.

The Austrian bishops said the encyclical didn't speak of serious sin, so failure to follow it would not separate people from God. The Canadian bishops responded in a very earthy manner by observing that there may well be a conflict of duties. People are faced with taking care of love, life, children, health, and so they should handle conception like any other value decisions; they should weigh the options, protect as many values as possible, and make a decision. They concluded with the statement that whoever honestly chooses the course seems right to him or her, does so in good conscience. The French bishops reverted to the moral discernment of centuries by saying that traditional wisdom always provides for seeking before God which duty is greater.

The interpretation of the teaching of the encyclical was also modified after further study of the text itself. There are two styles within the encyclical itself. One style is very pastoral, which is believed to have been written by Pope Paul himself. The other style is very exact, accurate, and demanding. It is as though Pope Paul felt he must hold up the traditional ideal of no artificial birth control, although he forgave those who could not live up to this ideal.

Without question, Pope Paul VI agonized a great deal over his encyclical. Some theologians who were personal friends opposed his stance. He never asked them to retract their position. As in all controversial matters, people's statements inevitably have qualifying clauses that are usually not quoted by secular news reporters or religious extremists. One of the statements of the encyclical, presumed to be written by the pope in his agony, was "and if sin [not specified] should still keep its hold over them [those with the problem of birth control], let them not be discouraged but rather have recourse with humble perseverence to the mercy of God which is put forth in the Sacrament of Penance." Eventually many confessors used this statement as justification for allowing people to continue using birth control in good conscience.

Though Pius XII had stated that birth control was intrinsically evil, and this seemed to be intimated by the encyclical *Humanae Vitae*, something happened that nobody dreamed of. Some nuns in Africa wrote to the Sacred Congregation in Rome asking if, since they were in real danger of being raped, they could protect themselves with contraception. The Sacred Congregation not only responded affirmatively, but even gave them instructions in the types of contraception that could be used, stating that it would be bad enough to be raped, but it would be far worse to be pregnant. As soon as Rome's response was made known to the theological world, the credibility gap widened between Rome's announced position on one hand and its contradiction when practical necessity called for common sense on the other—especially in an unrevealed matter. Following this, a group of visiting home nurses spoke up and said, "If those nuns think they're in danger, take a look at our position. We are in constant danger. Could we wear a diaphragm in case we're raped?"

In these examples and others, there was a profound silence in defense of the encyclical.

In Phoenix, Arizona, some years ago a priest of the diocesan senate expressed his fury to the bishop over the latter's editorial on *Humanae Vitae* in the Catholic paper. He was angry because the bishop quoted all the severe passages of the encyclical and omitted all the pastoral ones.

The priest presented the case of a woman with six children who was told by her doctor that her uterus was now perforated. Any further conception would most likely be disastrous to her and her conceived child. The bishop responded that he would advise her to use the sympto-thermal (rhythm) method. The priest fired back that she was irregular and the last two children were conceived by that method. He asked insistently, "Now what, bishop?" The bishop conceded that he was to inform her that she was allowed to use her own conscience in this matter.

With that response, the priest took a deep breath and, fighting to control himself, said to the bishop: "Some of you bishops are so frightened. While worrying about Rome, you fail to be pastoral. I have been given the exact same answer from another bishop. I hate these backroom decisions. Why didn't you print that in your editorial and give dignity instead of more agony to the prayerful judgment of thousands of women of your own diocese? Since you won't tell the whole truth, I'm going to write a rebuttle to your editorial."

The bishop did permit the rebuttal to be written.

Toward the end of the seventies a very thorough sociological study was done by Andrew Greeley on the position of the clergy on the birth control issue. He divided the priests into age categories. Priests between the ages of twenty-five and thirty-five were in one category, in another were ages thirty-five to forty-five, then an older group, and finally the oldest priests. He also polled religious superiors, heads of congregations, and bishops. Across the board, with the exception of the bishops, all age groups moved toward a more liberal approach to birth control. In this survey, four out of five priests in the category under thirty-five saw birth control as a nonissue. At the beginning of the eighties, another survey revealed that the vast majority of all priests consider it a nonissue.

A study was done on women in 1977 entitled "The Secularization of the United States Catholic Birth Control Practices." The survey demonstrate that except for sterilization, Catholic and non-Catholic contraceptive practices were quite similar. The survey projected that within several years even sterilization will probably be adopted by the same portions of Catholics and non-Catholics. It said the rhythm method is destined to be of historical interest. The wide gulf between official Catholic teaching and birth control behavior of Catholics would only deepen in the next few years. This has certainly taken place in reality.

In the mid-sixties the commission originally called by Pope John to study the unrevealed matter of birth control was eighty-five percent in favor of responsible parenthood that involved artificial birth control, the IUD excepted. If a poll of the entire Church was taken at the beginning of the eighties, the percentage in favor of birth control would probably be the same.

The debate is still not over. In a brilliant pastoral principally addressing the abortion issue, Cardinal Bernadin emphasizes the importance of a consistent ethic. We must look at all related issues when addressing the question of abortion.

The Church cannot ignore the fact that in places where birth control is still avoided in the United States among Catholics, there are more abortions for Catholics than for Protestants. The Catholic countries of Poland and Italy, where birth control is illegal, have the highest abortion rates in all of Europe. It seems more than evident that the most sincere and intelligent human proclamations of the official Church will come back to haunt us.

## HUMAN DIGNITY

It is not by accident or the absence of the Holy Spirit that in our the century where rigidity and absolutism have reigned in the field of moral pronouncements that the fourth greatest document on human liberty was composed. Not only was it composed in our century, but it was one of the Vatican documents formulated by the best theologians of the Church, purified by debate and research, and signed by all the bishops and the pope of the Second Vatican Council. Though it is hard to stop the harm that is created by the rigidity and absolutism of religious, righteous people, clerical or lay, the Roman Catholic Church has officially made a statement against them.

Many who have been broken by the human events of life, or even sin, can be brought to the ultimate joy of still following the teaching Church by reading *Dignitatis Humanae Personae,* considered the greatest document of religious freedom in all the history of the Catholic Church. Pope Paul VI called it one of the major texts of the entire council. This document goes beyond Saint Thomas's discussion of the right of each human being to decide his or her own position before God, even in the Church. Anyone who opposes that right, pastor or parent, is opposing the teaching of the Church.

Although the the entire document must be read before experiencing its full joy of religious freedom, a few paragraphs might reflect its faith in the human being and his or her judgment:

A person has been made by God to participate in this law, with the result that, under the gentle disposition of divine Providence, he or she can come to perceive ever increasingly the enchanging truth. Hence every person has the duty, and therefore the right, to seek the truth in matters religious, in order that he or she may with prudence form for himself or herself right and true judgments of conscience, with the use of all suitable means.

On his or her part, a person perceives and acknowledges the imperatives of the divine law through the medication of conscience. In all activity a person is bound to follow his or her own conscience faithfully, in order that he or she may come to God, for whom he or she was created. It follows that he or she is not to be forced to act in a manner contrary to his or her conscience. Nor, on the other hand, is he or she to be restrained from acting in accordance with his or her conscience, especially in matters religious.

There is an interesting story about the principal author of this document, John Courtney Murray, S.J. Because of his stance on human freedom and religious liberty, he had earlier been forbidden to speak in virtually every diocese of the United States. A directive from Rome demanded that he cease writing. Very obediently Father Murray took all of his research books from his room to the library at Woodstock, New York. Then when the Second Vatican Council began, he was called to Rome to fashion the document. A few years after its completion and publication as part of the treasury of the Catholic Church, John Courtney Murray died. It was then that cardinals, archbishops, bishops, monsignori, and priests from all over attended the funeral in his honor. It took the Church's approval to soften the rigidity of many of their hearts.

# 6. A Vital Ministry: The Ministries and Organizations for the Divorced and Remarried

While controversy reigns in the halls of higher learning about absolute indissolubility, covenant/contract, sacramentality, concepts of consummation, and the morality of the annulment process, outside on the front porch sobs a victim of divorce asking a more profound question than the scholars: "to be or not to be?" We turn our attention now to the real and existential ministry of the Church.

## SUPPORT GROUPS

Support groups are the most effective ministries in the Christian community for the separated and divorced. Such groups allow individuals to work through the stages of disbelief, anger, revenge, craziness, and recovery.[33] It is one of the most healing ministries because it vents emotions and deters irrational actions of the one suffering. But those involved in this kind of ministry can expect to be criticized frequently.

It is an important ministry because often divorce terminates a sick relationship that has been deteriorating for years and the results are very ugly. Yet so often when a divorced person recovers and is willing to get on with life again, he or she moves out of the group and does not stay to listen to the hurt of others. Such groups accelerate the recovery time of a divorced person by months or even a year or so.

Support groups are the best tool for preventing rebound marriages. It is estimated that sixty percent of all the people who are divorced are remarried within one year. Twenty percent more are remarried within the second year. Yet an estimated three to four years is necessary for the average person to recover from a divorce. It is no wonder, then, that the divorce rate in second marriages is three to four percent higher than the divorce rate in first marriages. Many divorced people resent the concept of a long recovery time. For those who have been separated or estranged for many years, obviously, recovery time after actual divorce may be shorter. This is not true for those who are raw from the experience.

A year seems to be the amount of time needed to experience life without "reacting" after a divorce. Even in estrangement, holidays, Christmas, Thanksgiving, birthdays, and vacations bring on the challenge of including or excluding the former spouse. Another year of human experience leads the person who has really interiorized his or her aloneness to the discovery of a personal identity that may have been lost in a hurting marriage relationship. A person may discover that he or she does not like the personality developed by reacting to the former spouse for so many years. By opening the door to new people and experiences, and perhaps through counseling, recovery takes place. It is then that the divorced person might consider another marriage relationship.

Our culture has a prejudice against the single state, yet it teaches independence and self-fulfillment. Almost all advertising in the commercial world portrays love and companionship in a courting or married context. Many marry who should remain single. In the annulment process it is revealed often that in many cases social pressure caused the couple to marry. Those who are able to endure the requisite recovery time after divorce often discover that the single life is more appropriate for them. Unfortunately they did not realize that prior to entering marriage.

Today many couples live together prior to marriage. Most of the couples resent the term "trial marriage." It is a trial, however, for establishing mutual compatibility. The irony of this trial period is that a commitment is necessary to work out many personal differences between two people. Without a permanent commitment a person may suppress sensitive communication and even deviant behavior patterns out of fear of losing the lover. Many such relationships end in divorce shortly after the marriage because the one of the partners has now been "hooked."

Sometimes couples in a trial relationship separate before marriage and the effects of this separation on them are closely akin to the effects on divorced persons. The term "separated" now designates not only those who are separated in a marriage but also those who have terminated a trial marriage of a few or many years. Trial marriages have resulted in a noticeable population who do not want to commit themselves in marriage; they want the physical and psychic pleasure of a companion without marital responsibility. The personal devastation can even be more acute for those separated from a trial marriage than those separated from a marriage of commitment.

## SPIRITUAL DIRECTION

When the field is plowed, it is ready to be planted. Such is the position of many of those who have divorced. Endless numbers of divorced Catholics became deeply religious people after the feeling of being broken from their separation. There are many different aspects to this particular process of faith through tragedy. For the first time many are able to take a mature look at their faith teaching, especially the moral instructions of the Church. People who have been through a divorce are far less "righteous" than standard parochial Catholics. Because of misconceptions, shattered self-image, shame, confusion, and hate, divorced people often alienate themselves from any religious community and/or religious standards.

This separation from familiar religious places and practices brings about the sense of loss of religion. This sense of loss brings with it, especially after recovery, a profound sense of what religious standards and community have really meant in a person's life. People often leave a childish or adolescent practice of religion and develop a very sensitive awareness of what religion should be doing for people. Many, too, are totally unaware of the resources within the Catholic community for those who need spiritual, social, legal, and even medical help. Many a divorced person has found religious identification far more enriched by questioning, challenging, and demanding rather than being a mute spectator at a Sunday liturgy. For the vast number of religious people, self-imposed penance is the principal means of identifying with the sufferings of Christ. Even a casual glance at the New Testament reveals that Jesus' suffering was predominately other-inflicted. He was the victim. Perhaps no one can understand this type of redemptive suffering more than a divorced person who is a victim of life's circumstances.

## MINISTRY

There has always been an awareness in the Christian tradition of the power of like ministering to like. "Wounded healers" are particularly effective because they have experienced what they are attempting to help with. This ministry to the divorced and separated by the divorced and separated has become one of the most powerful movements of ministry in the Catholic Church of America today. Literally hundreds of different support groups have been spawned and flourish throughout the United States.

Probably the most recognized of all the groups is the Association of Formerly Married Catholics. This organization was formed when a spunky group of lay people asked a priest, James Young, what the Church was doing for the divorced. He insightfully redirected the question to them. The organization was then founded that involves thousands across the nation today. The national and regional conferences of the AFMC have had the stature to call forth spectacular talent for the care and the direction of the divorced and remarried.

Following on the heels of this nationally proclaimed organization came the Beginning Experience, founded by Sister Josephine Stewart, S.S.M.N. Out of the highly successful format of the Cursillo and Marriage Encounter, the Beginning Experience became a soul-searching experience that brings the divorced and separated to accept their own responsibility in the marriage breakup, get in touch with their own power to forgive themselves and their former spouses, and say goodbye to the past in order to live life to the full in the present. The utterly blunt and no-nonsense witnessing on the part of these wounded healers has prompted many divorced and separated individuals to abandon their grief and helplessness and to become vibrant enough to inspire other people to get on with productive lives. A wide variety of other support groups have been formed by restless divorced people who have asked the question, "What is the Church doing for us?"

It is imperative that the wounds from the previous marriage are healed, forgiveness of the former spouse is complete, and the person has said a firm goodbye to the former relationship before accepting another. The number of divorces after remarriage is higher than among those who are leaving a first marriage. Often the second marriage is still contaminated by the first. In dealing with the divorced or separated person, a priest or minister must inquire concerning the just fulfillment of all the responsibilities resulting from the first marriage, including child support, property, or family connections. The unsettled ghosts of the past have a mysterious way of haunting the present.

## HEALING THE BAD MEMORIES

For some, time heals; people get tired of hurting. For others, time does not heal—ministry heals; working through the hurt heals; understanding heals. Support groups afford a divorced person a caring community in which he or she can accelerate the healing process.[34] But support groups can help only so much when divorce is a symptom of some deeper personality dysfunction. In these cases the people are not necessarily psychotic. They may only have an attitude toward life or a personality characteristic that needs more accurate treatment by professional help. In such cases, divorce might well be the beginning of life and freedom for an individual. Psychological counseling can often focus on and locate the disabling quality in a person that contributed to the divorce.

## DISCERNMENT

No two automobile accident are the same. This is even more true of human accidents. If a person goes to a doctor with an illness and complains, "I hurt," the obvious response would be "Where?" This should be the response of someone who ministers to the divorced and separated. The search for healing should begin with two questions: "What are you feeling?" and "What prompts the feeling?" Since each individual is a many splendored mystery, these two questions should be asked again and again in the discernment process of what the divorce tragedy truly means to an individual.

There are two sets of emotions, one for "the leaver" and one for "the left." The leaver may experience feelings of failure, betrayal, fear, disgust, hate, relief, joy, care, and even love. The leaver always has an element of control. This lessens the victim complex. For "the left," the range of reactions may include fright, thoughts about suicide, numbness, inadequacy, shame, rejection, hate, disgust, and even at times relief or satisfaction. The very nature of this position lacks control. The feeling of being a victim is experienced far more by "the left" than by "the leaver."

Depending upon a divorced person's background, the aids in recovery may come from areas of religion, psychology, or social interaction. Most of the time it is a combination of all three.

Death and divorce are generally rated among the top five on the Richter scale of human experiences. Because of the profound nature of divorce, people have a tendency to scatter their resources of recovery. This generally produces greater exhaustion and lengthens the time of recovery.[35] The one who provides the catalyst for discernment in the divorced or separated person is the one who accelerates recovery and turns pain into growth and wisdom.

On the other hand, those who cut an individual off with the clichés—"I know exactly how you feel," "It's probably better that it happened," "It's the will of God," "Pull yourself together,"—add further injury to an already painful situation and cause further confusion. Ask What does this mean to you?" and the person going through this powerful life reorientation has a chance to vent that pent-up misery. Just allowing a person to breathe from their spirit world is healing in itself.

## REASSURANCE

People who sensitively deal with death and divorce are often at a loss as to how to properly respond to a particularly tragic moment in someone's life. Tragedy instantly brings out the complex meaning of an individual's hopes and dreams and passions and loves. At the moment of impact, some go into shock; they are too stunned to decipher anything. Sometimes the best response is just to hug them or say "I love you." Reassuring them that someone will be with them throughout the ordeal can bring the much-needed hope for survival to someone staggering under the weight of tragedy.[36]

## FRIENDS

It is often observed that in a time of tragedy a person finds out who his or her true friends are. While this is true, sometimes friends are not the best help. The bond of love may be so encompassing that a real friend is likewise paralyzed. Furthermore, some friends can be a liability with their enthusiasm to make things right. Some of the worst counselors are close friends. Objectivity is clouded by the closeness of the relationship.

A true friend, however, might be able to point out any peculiar behavior patterns taken on while dealing with agony of divorce or even the activity of the former spouse. An honest, listening, accepting, supportive friend is the strongest get-well medicine in the complete experience of human life.

The powerful emotions of anger, disillusionment, and bitterness of a newly separated or divorced person can make unreasonable demands on friends. The divorced person often asks of bridge companions to be emotionally discerning. And some people are not in touch with their own interior spirit, much less able to help with someone else's.

Divorced people can be repetious in their narration of the breakup. Though sometimes aggravating for friends, it is necessary that the divorced person both vent the hurt and come to terms with what has occurred. After the first impact of the separation wears off, self-centeredness is often the necessary next stage. Often the divorced are insulted if they are reminded that the story is a repeat of what was narrated an hour before, but such repetition is often a sign of the depth of the anguish and the necessity to "work through" a severe trauma.

Self-pity can be self-nurturing, especially in the beginning. However, if self-pity goes beyond nine months or a year, recovery is delayed and responsibility for life is avoided.

Divorced people will sometimes feel compelled to tell their story over and over again to clergy too. Since clergy are limited in time and energy, a group setting of divorced people is an efficient way of allowing them to tell their stories over and over again until some healing can take place.

CONCLUSION

The musical *The Flower Drum Song* tells the story of a man who would not wait for the gradual development of the growth of the butterfly. In his impatience he opened the wings of the butterfly before they had time to unfurl themselves. This impatience killed the butterfly.

Divorce has been a part of human life since the origin of relationships. It is extremely rare for someone to enter a marriage with the purpose of divorcing; divorce is not intended by those marrying. Yet it occurs and nature itself is an overwhelming witness that for many living creatures the birth of freedom takes place only through pain. The insight of the Christian tradition is that to those who believe, all things, even divorce, can work unto good.

# Notes

1. James Provost, "Intolerable Marriage Situations Revisited," *The Jurist* 40 (1980): 1, 155.
2. Anthony McDevitt, "Divorce and the Eucharist," *Catholic Mind* (May 1977): 45.
3. Provost, "Intolerable Marriage Situations Revisited," 149.
4. Joseph Zwack, *Annulment: Your Chance to Remarry Within the Catholic Church* (New York: Harper & Row, 1983), 73.
5. Dale Alfred Patrick, "A Study of Conceptual Model of the Covenant, (Ph. D. diss., University of California, Berkeley, 1971).
6. Ralph Tapia, "Divorce and Remarriage in the Catholic Church Today," *Thought* (September 1982): 386.
7. Lawrence Wrenn, *Divorce and Remarriage in the Catholic Church* (New York: Newman Press, 1973), 3.
8. Theodore Mackin, S.J., *What Is Marriage?* (New York: Paulist Press, 1982), 42.
9. Wrenn, *Divorce and Remarriage in the Catholic Church*, 8–9.
10. Joseph Martos, *Doors to the Sacred* (New York: Image Books, 1982), 400.
11. Mackin, *What Is Marriage?*, 77.
12. Martos, *Doors to the Sacred*, 407.
13. Ibid., 408–409.
14. Mackin, *What Is Marriage?*, 77.
15. Martos, *Doors to the Sacred*, 416.
16. Mackin, *What Is Marriage?*, 78.
17. Martos, *Doors to the Sacred*, 421.
18. Ibid., 422.
19. Ibid.
20. Mackin, *What Is Marriage?*, 148–149.
21. Ibid., 155.
22. Martos, *Doors to the Sacred*, 437.
23. Theodore Davey, "Alternatives to Nullity Procedures," *Month* (November 1980): 366.
24. James Cuneo, "The Judge as Expert," *The Jurist* 42 (1982): 1, 146.
25. Tapia, "Divorce and Remarriage in the Catholic Church Today," 393.
26. Gerald Coleman, "The Internal Forum Solution," *The Priest* (January 1983): 34.
27. Davey, "Alternatives to Nullity Procedures," 366.
28. Tapia, "Divorce and Remarriage in the Catholic Church Today," 385.
29. Excerpt from a letter by the Sacred Congregation in Rome addressed to Archbishop Bernardin, March 21, 1985.
30. Provost, "Intolerable Marriage Situations Revisited," 44.
31. Tapia, "Divorce and Remarriage in the Catholic Church Today," 385.

32. IV SENTENCES, dist. 38, a.4.
33. Paula Ripple, F.S.P.A., *The Pain and the Possibility* (Notre Dame, IN: Ave Maria Press, 1978), 44.
34. James Young, *Ministering to the Divorced Catholic* (New York: Paulist Press, 1979), 129.
35. Ibid., 173.
36. Ibid., 183.

# Bibliography

## BOOKS

de Margerie, Bertrand. *Remarried Divorcées and Eucharistic Communion*. Boston: Daughters of St. Paul, 1980.

Kelleher, Stephen J. *Divorce and Remarriage for Catholics?* New York: Alba House, 1975.

Mackin, Theodore, S.J. *What is Marriage?* New York, Paulist Press, 1982.

Martos, Joseph. *Doors to the Sacred*. New York: Image Books, 1982.

McCormick, Richard, S.J. *Notes on Moral Theology 1965 through 1980*. Washington: University Press of America, 1981.

Noonan, John T., Jr. *Power to Dissolve*. Cambridge, MA: Harvard University, Press, Belknap Press, 1972.

Ripple, Paula, F.S.P.A. *The Pain and the Possibility*. Notre Dame, IN: Ave Maria Press, 1978.

Thomas, John L. *The American Catholic Family*. Greenwood, 1980.

Tierney, Terence. *Annulment: Do You Have a Case?* New York: Alba House, 1978.

Twomey, Gerald. *When Catholics Marry Again*. Minneapolis, MN: Winston Press, 1982.

Westermarck, Edward. *The History of Human Marriage*. London: Macmillan, 1921.

Wrenn, Lawrence. *Annulments*. Rev. ed. Toledo, OH: Canon Law Society of America, 1978.

———. *Divorce and Remarriage in the Catholic Church*. New York: Newman Press, 1973.

Young, James. *Divorce Ministry and the Marriage Tribunal*. New York: Paulist Press, 1982.

———. *Ministering to the Divorced Catholic*. New York: Paulist Press, 1979.

Zwack, Joseph P. *Annulment: Your Chance to Remarry Within the Catholic Church*. New York: Harper & Row, 1983.

## ARTICLES

Bernhard, Jean. "The Evolution of Matrimonial Jurisprudence: The Opinion of a French Canonist." *The Jurist*, 41 (1981):1, pp. 105–116.

Bourke, Myles. "An Exegesis of the Divorce Tests in the New Testament." *Diakonia* 4 (1961): 39–44.

Coleman, Gerald. "The Internal Forum Solution." *The Priest* (January 1983): 33–36.

Cuneo, James. "The Judge as Expert." *The Jurist,* 42 (1982):1, pp. 141–163.

Davey, Theodore. "Alternatives to Nullity Procedures." *Month* (November 1980): 365–370.

———. "Divorce: the State of the Question Within the Catholic Church." *Month* (June 1981): 185–190.

Donahue, John. "Divorce: New Testament Perspective." *Month* (April 1981): 113–120.

Fogarty, Gerald. "The Historical Origin of the Excommunication of Divorced and Remarried Catholics Imposed by the Third Plenary Council of Baltimore." *The Jurist,* 30 (1978): 426–433.

Hughes, John J. "Hebrew 9:15 ††: a Study in Covenant Practice and Procedure." *Novum Testamentum* 21 (January 1979): 27–96.

McDevitt, Anthony. "Divorce and the Eucharist." *Catholic Mind* (May 1977): 44–51.

Oglesby, William. "Divorce and Remarriage in Christian Perspective." *Pastoral Psychology* (Summer 1977): 282–293.

Palmer, Paul, S.J. "Christian Marriage: Contract or Covenant?" *Theological Studies* 33 (December 1972): 617–665.

———. "When a Marriage Dies." *America* 12 (February 1975): 126–128.

Patrick, Dale Alfred. "A Study of Conceptual Model of the Covenant." Ph. D. dissertation, University of California at Berkeley, 1971.

Provost, James. "Intolerable Marriage Situations Revisited." *The Jurist* 40 (1980):1, pp. 141–196.

Seward, Desmond. "Divorce, an Obstacle in the Catholic-Orthodox Dialogue." *The Dublin Review* (Spring 1966): 154–160.

Tapia, Ralph. "Divorce and Remarriage in the Roman Catholic Church Today." *Thought* (September 1982): 179–204.

Urrutia, Francisco, S.J. "The Internal Forum Solution–Some Comments." *The Jurist,* 40 (1980):1, pp. 128–140.

Valentine, Peter. "Divorce, Remarriage, and the Sacraments." *The Jurist,* 42 (1982):1, pp. 122–140.

Van der Poel, Cornelius. "Influences of an Annulment Mentality." *The Jurist,* 40 (1980):2, pp. 384–399.

Whelan, Charles. "Divorced Catholics: A Proposal." *America* (7 December 1974): 363–366.

# Appendix: Directory of Support Groups

THE BEGINNING EXPERIENCE

AUSTRALIA

Brisbane
Joan Mason
1/183 Fernberg Rd.
Paddington, 4064
Queensland
Australia

Melbourne
Lyn Rogers
6 Ryong St.
Grovedale
Victoria 3216
Australia
052-437777

Sydney
Ron Stevens
221 Old Kent Rd.
Greenacre 2190
Australia
774-1721

CANADA

Calgary
Sherrie Grace
10813 5 St., S.W.
Calgary
Alberta T2W 1W5
Canada
(403) 252-5782

Prince Edward Island
Jean Blanchard
138 Upper Prince Street
Charlottetown, P.E.I.
Canada C1A 4S7
(902) 894-3510

Sarnia
Jane Danic
1069 London Road
Sarnia, Ontario
Canada N7T 5V4
(508) 344-0771

Winnipeg
Bob Dick
500 Hargrave St.
Winnipeg, Manitoba
Canada R3A 0X7
(204) 257-1161

NEW ZEALAND

Auckland
Patrick Hallissey
53 Glen Rd.
Devonport, Auckland
New Zealand

Christchurch
Val Quinn
25 Pegasus Ave.
Christchurch 9
New Zealand

UNITED STATES
ALABAMA

Birmingham
Kathleen Hertrich
2429 Vale Drive
Birmingham, AL 35244
(205) 988-0863

Mobile
Sara Scheer
1922 LaPine Dr.
Mobile, AL 36618
(205) 344-2106

ALASKA

Anchorage
Lynn Sampson
13405 WindRush Circle
Anchorage, AK 99516
(907) 345-7299

Fairbanks
Fr. Timothy Sander
Fairbanks Counseling & Adopt.
P.O. Box 1544
Fairbanks, AK 99707
(907) 456-4729

ARIZONA

Phoenix — Fr. Val Boyle, O.Carm.
1717 West Flower
Phoenix, AZ 85015
(602) 274-0442

Tucson — Dino Natta
600 E. River Rd. #E
Tucson, AZ 85704
(602) 888-6482

ARKANSAS

Little Rock — Connie Flanery
Route 2, Box 443
Dover, Arkansas
72837
(501) 967-3004

CALIFORNIA

East Bay Area — Barbara Shultz
3320 Noyo St.
Oakland, CA
94602
(415) 531-1100

Los Angeles — Mary Kay Crowther
351 Linares Avenue
Long Beach, CA
90803
(213) 598-5639

Monterey Bay — Jan Schultz
423 Pleasant Valley Rd.
Aptos, CA 95003
(408) 722-9902

San Bernardino — Stevie Leppard
320 Manzanita
Rialto, CA 92376
(714) 824-9326

San Diego — Brian Davis
3669 Calavo Dr.
Spring Valley, CA
92077
(619) 560-5799

San Jose — Marian Escobar
21030 Canyon View Dr.
Saratoga, CA
95070
(408) 867-1848

Santa Barbara — Patricia A. Grattan
1085 Estrella Dr.
Santa Barbara, CA
93110
(805) 682-3271

COLORADO

Colorado Springs — Sue Adamic
1432 Chestnut
Canon City, CO
81212
(303) 275-2952

Denver — Loren Livermore
1335 Dover St.
Broomfield, CO
80020
(303) 466-6217

Durango — Alice Herod
29251 Hwy. 160
Durango, CO
81301
(303) 247-9768

Fort Collins — Betty Ellis
1205 Hillcrest Dr.
Fort Collins, CO
80521
(303) 493-9150

DISTRICT OF COLUMBIA

Baltimore/D.C./ Wilmington — Carrie Hanson
800 Downs Dr.
Silver Springs, MD
20904
(301) 622-4421

FLORIDA

Miami — Sr. Agnes Gott
Family Enrichment Ctr.
18330 N.W. 12th Ave.
Miami, FL 33169
(305) 651-0280

GEORGIA

Atlanta — Rosemary O'Boyle
3909 Briar Glen Ct.
Atlanta, GA 30340
(404) 493-3909

**HAWAII**

Oahu/ Lorraine Busekrus
Honolulu 206 Akai Street
Kihei, HI 96753
(808) 879-2422

**IDAHO**

Boise Cathy Burgess
7034 Hummel Drive
Boise, ID 83709
(208) 322-6226

**ILLINOIS**

Chicago, N&W Emelia Alberico
16056 Woodlawn
East
South Holland, IL
60473
(312) 339-4100

Chicago S. Charlotte Ratcliffe
1301 West 71st
Place
Chicago, IL 60636
(312) 994-0209

Peoria Melody Tidwell
110 Jade Court
Washington, IL
61571
(309) 745-8671

Rockford Patricia Story
1722 Tacoma
Avenue
Rockford, IL 61103
(815) 965-3929

**INDIANA**

Fort Wayne Elizabeth Merkler
2834 Grandview
Dr.
Fort Wayne, IN
46804
(219) 432-1683

Indianapolis Leonard Bibeau
4233 Broadway
Indianapolis, IN
46205
(317) 283-1690

Lafayette Karen Holland
2521 Cayuga Trail
Lafayette, IN
46905
(317) 474-3634

South Bend Janet Reed
18060 Bariger Place
South Bend, IN 46637
(219) 277-1955

**IOWA**

Des Moines Ellen Perez
525—7th
West Des Moines, IA
50265
(515) 279-4717

Dubuque/ Judy Hosch
Davenport 805 7th Ave. S.E.
Dyerville, IA 52040
(319) 875-2261

Sioux City Rev. James A. Bruch
2223 Indian Hills
Sioux City, IA 51104
(712) 255-7933

**KANSAS**

Kansas City Alice Cribelar
Route 2, Box 411
Monsees Lake Estates
Sedalia, MO 65301
(816) 827-5617

Wichita Fr. Paul Oborny
638 Avenue D. West
Kingman, KS 67068
(316) 532-5440

**KENTUCKY**

Louisville Julie W. Zoeller
511 Drawbrook Circle
New Albany, IN
47150
(812) 948-9942

**LOUISIANA**

Baton Rouge Pat Thomas
8960 Cedar Glen
Baton Rouge, LA
70811
(504) 355-1393

New Orleans Drucy Fisk
4929 Zenith St.
Metairie, LA 70001
(504) 887-8302

Shreveport Kay Sears
2038 Pitch Pine Drive
Shreveport, LA
71118
(318) 687-0237

**MASSACHUSETTS**

Boston
Fredda Megan
9 Claire Dr.
Attleboro, MA
02703
(617) 222-5907

Springfield
Jean Czajka
157 Rimmon Ave.
Chicopee, MA
01013
(413) 594-2397

**MICHIGAN**

Detroit
Ardelle Spiewak
911 Vernier
Grosse Pointe
Woods, MI 48236
(313) 885-6287

Flint
Hetty Coe
4421 Carmanwood
Drive
Flint, MI 48507
(313) 238-8279

Lansing
Janice Atwell
416 E. Kalamo
Hwy.
Charlotte, MI
48813
(517) 543-8329

Traverse City
Dori Obuchowski
118 S. Spruce St.
Traverse City, MI
49684
(616) 947-2348

**MINNESOTA**

Alexandria
Marilyn Tisserand
Rt. 1, Box 143-A
Garfield, MN
56332
(612) 834-2100

Crookston
Shirley Melander
Route 4, Box 152
Frazee, MN 56544
(218) 334-5302

Duluth
Leanne Smith
1410 Martin Road
Duluth, MN 55803
(218) 736-0057

Mankato
Pam Willard
225 Locke
Mankato, MN
56001
(507) 338-6621

Marshall Area/
SW Minn.
Carol Orthaus
1305 Greenview
Place
Marshall, MN
56258
(507) 532-6614

Minneapolis/
St. Paul
Karleen Parnell
1968 Stanford
St. Paul, MN 55105
(612) 699-3778

Rochester
Helen McBride
1210 4 1/2 St.
NW
Rochester, MN
55901
(507) 288-7791

St. Cloud Area/
Central MN
Sr. Kate Casper
305 N. 7th Ave.,
Suite 100
St. Cloud, MN
56301
(612) 252-4121

**MISSOURI**

St. Louis/
Belleville
Lucille Bedan
745 Glenvista Place
Glendale, MO
63122
(314) 968-3568

Cape Girardeau
Charlotte Hooper
Rt. 1, Box 1434
Scott City, MO
63780
(314) 968-3568

**NEBRASKA**

North Platte
Joe Stieb
4400 Rodeo Rd.
North Platte, NE
69101
(308) 534-6212

Omaha
Betty
Meinershagen
5516 North 63
Street
Omaha, NE 68104
(402) 571-5806

**NEVADA**

Las Vegas
Anne Anderson
603 Spyglass
Las Vegas, NV
89107
(702) 878-6715

**NEW JERSEY**

Lafayette Frank Padden
8 Kimble Lane
Sparta, NJ 07871
(201) 383-4565

**NEW MEXICO**

Albuquerque Patricia Martin
2523 Stevens N.E.
Albuquerque, NM
87112
(505) 298-7035

**NEW YORK**

Buffalo Susan Murray
222 School Road
Kenmore, NY 14217
(716) 873-7946

Long Island Peter D'Aguanno
5 Sargent Place
Manhasset, NY
11030
(516) 365-7683

Brooklyn/ Gina Colelli
Queens 117–14 Union Tpke.
Kew Gardens, NY
11227
(718) 544-4753

Rochester Judy Markowski
4403 Cream Ridge
Macedon, NY 14502
(315) 524-8649

Syracuse Patricia MacDonald
164 Marshland Rd.
Apalachin, NY 13732
(607) 625-3057

**NORTH DAKOTA**

Bismarck Richard Silvernagel
2414 Winchester Dr.
Bismarck, ND
58501
(701) 258-3197

Fargo Fr. Wendy Vetter
P.O. Box 1750
Fargo, ND 58107
(701) 293-7722

**OHIO**

Cincinnati Judy Carcifero
3555 Epley Rd.
Cincinnati, OH
45247
(513) 385-0360

Cleveland Rose Marie Parisi
12688 Islandview
Dr., N.W.
Uniontown, OH
O44685
(216) 699-4341

Columbus Peter Andersen
5354 Woodglen
Road
Columbus, OH
43214
(614) 431-5191

Dayton Julie Kinarney
4054 Quail Bush
Dr.
Dayton, OH 45424
(513) 236-1959

Toledo Dolly Lake
1765 South St.
Millbury, OH 43447
(419) 855-7522

Youngstown Judy Isenberg
844 Pleasant Dr.
Warren, OH 44483
(216) 847-0842

**OKLAHOMA**

Lawton Betty Hall
36 S.W. 45 St.
Lawton, OK 73505
(405) 357-1155

Oklahoma City Warren Luce
425 N.W. 25th #6
Oklahoma City, OK
73103
(405) 528-3510

**OREGON**

Portland/ Jim Karle
Salem 9922 SW 30th
Portland, OR 97219
(503) 246-0219

**PENNSYLVANIA**

Scranton Steffe Berdy
7 York Ave.
Towanda, PA 18848
(717) 265-2679

**SOUTH DAKOTA**

Sioux Falls/ Doris O'Dea
Eastern Area 503 S. Glendale
Sioux Falls, SD
57104
(605) 334-4131

Rapid City/ Western Area
Mary Burns
1702 E. Hwy. 44
#22
Rapid City, SD
57701
(605) 341-1575

**TEXAS**

Amarillo
Connie Rickwartz
3224 Janet, #107
Amarillo, TX 79109
(806) 358-9202

Austin
Vern Dawson
306 Ridgewood Dr.
Georgetown, TX
78626
(512) 863-8227

Beaumont
Mary Ethelyn
Bosarge
907 Shaw Dr.
Nederland, TX
77627
(409) 727-2576

Corpus Christi
Betty Buhidar
1701 Thames #113
Corpus Christ, TX
78412
(512) 991-2780

Dallas/ Ft. Worth
Clovis Cazale
518 Lexington Lane
Richardson, TX
75080
(214) 231-2012

El Paso
Rosie Torres
7312 Benson Dr.
El Paso, TX 79915
(915) 592-3956

Houston
Margaret Garcia
3809 Canterbury
Baytown, TX 77521
(713) 428-7419

Houston-Episcopal Expression
Lolita J. McColley
16326 Quail Echo Dr.
Missouri City, TX
77489
(713) 438-1348

Rio Grande Valley
Lois Speaker
2314 E. Monroe
Harlingen, TX
78550
(512) 423-9160

San Antonio
Mary White
8258 Campobello
San Antonio, TX
78218
(512) 657-5172

**WASHINGTON**

Seattle
Betty Wolfe
4806 E. Mercer Way
Mercer Island, WA
98040
(206) 232-2849

Spokane
Mike Samuel
N. 4907 Cook
Spokane, WA
99207
(509) 487-1563

Tacoma
Roger Koehn
38110 303rd S.E.
Enumclaw, WA
98022
(206) 825-1237

**WISCONSIN**

Green Bay/ Neenah
Kathy Geisler
1331 Bellevue, Lot 185
Green Bay, WI
54302
(414) 468-5728

Madison
Gail Lamberty
R.R. 2, Box 30
Sauk City, WI
53583
(608) 643-8017

Milwaukee
Penny D'Acquisto
1308 West Blvd.
Racine, WI 53402
(414) 637-3142

Superior
Sr. Eileen Lang
Christian Renewal
Center
Rt. 2, Box 388
Cameron, WI
54822
(715) 458-2922

**WYOMING**

Cheyenne
Judy Bannon
3935 Dorset Ct.
Casper, WY 82601
(307) 266-1067

# NORTH AMERICAN CONFERENCE OF SEPARATED AND DIVORCED CATHOLICS, INC.

## 1984–1985 EXECUTIVE BOARD

CENTRAL OFFICE
Kathleen L. Kircher
Executive Director
1100 S. Goodman St.
Rochester, NY 14620
(716) 271-1320

CHAPLAIN
Rev. James J. Young
3015 4th Street, N.E.
Washington, DC 20017
(202) 832-6262

CANADA
WESTERN CANADA
Beverly Susnir
26–287 Southampton Dr., S.W.
Calgary, Alberta T2W 2N5
(403) 255-5287

ONTARIO
Marjorie Moore
1314 Firestone Cresc.
Ottawa, Ontario K2C 3E3
(613) 828-5544

QUEBEC
Pia Stack
4892 Lake Road
Dollard Des Ormeaux
Quebec, Canada H9G 1G8
(514) 626-2032

UNITED STATES
REGION I
Maureen Rich
169 Haverhill St.
Reading, MA 01867
(617) 944-1882

REGION II
Patrick J. Letourneau
8521 Porter Rd., Apt. 129
Niagara Falls, NY 14304
(716) 297-5242

REGION III
Liz Barca
14 Overlook Ave.
West Orange, NJ 07052
(201) 731-2878

REGION IV
Caroline Mallett
6913 Hamilton Ct.
Lorton, VA 22079
(703) 550-7609

REGION V
Brian Dalton
P.O. Box 243
Hermitage, TN 37076
(615) 331-7333

REGION VI
Marie J. Loy
15847 Touraine Ct.
Mt. Clemens, MI 48044
(313) 263-4845

REGION VII
Judith C. McArdle
27 N. Cornell St.
Villa Park, IL 60181
(312) 941-0927

REGION VIII
Richard Bernard
P.O. Box 11
Hibbing, MN 55746
(218) 262-6454

REGION IX
Diane Giamarino
411 S. Geyer Rd., Apt. 1-B
St. Louis, MO 63122
(314) 821-3279

REGION X
Fred C. Eckhart, Jr.
6565 West Loop South
Suite #445
Bellaire, TX 77401
(713) 266-0411

REGION XI
Bobbi Coyle-Hennessey
6098 Guadalupe Mines Rd.
San Jose, CA 95120
(408) 268-0507

REGION XII
Connie Hanser
1992 Waldron Drive
Anchorage, AK 99507
(907) 563-7525

REGION XIII
Mary Ann Kristiansen
4321 Comanche Dr.
Laramie, WY 82070
(307) 742-3134

# INDEX